Mount Pleasant

Steve Poizner

Mount Pleasant

My Journey from Creating
a Billion-Dollar Company
to Teaching at a Struggling
Public High School

PORTFOLIO

PORTFOLIO
Published by the Penguin Group
Penguin Group (USA) Inc., 375 Hudson Street, New York, New York 10014, U.S.A.
Penguin Group (Canada), 90 Eglinton Avenue East, Suite 700, Toronto, Ontario, Canada M4P 2Y3
(a division of Pearson Penguin Canada Inc.)
Penguin Books Ltd, 80 Strand, London WC2R 0RL, England
Penguin Ireland, 25 St. Stephen's Green, Dublin 2, Ireland (a division of Penguin Books Ltd)
Penguin Books Australia Ltd, 250 Camberwell Road, Camberwell, Victoria 3124, Australia
(a division of Pearson Australia Group Pty Ltd)
Penguin Books India Pvt Ltd, 11 Community Centre, Panchsheel Park, New Delhi – 110 017, India
Penguin Group (NZ), 67 Apollo Drive, Rosedale, North Shore 0632, New Zealand
(a division of Pearson New Zealand Ltd)
Penguin Books (South Africa) (Pty) Ltd, 24 Sturdee Avenue, Rosebank, Johannesburg 2196, South Africa

Penguin Books Ltd, Registered Offices: 80 Strand, London WC2R 0RL, England

First published in 2010 by Portfolio,
a member of Penguin Group (USA) Inc.

10 9 8 7 6 5 4 3 2 1

LIBRARY OF CONGRESS CATALOGING IN PUBLICATION DATA
Poizner, Steve, 1957–
Mount Pleasant : my journey from creating a billion-dollar company to teaching at a struggling public high
school / Steve Poizner.
p. cm.
ISBN 978-1-59184-345-0
1. Poizner, Steve, 1957– 2. Businessmen—California—Biography. 3. Politicians—California—Biography.
4. Volunteer workers in education—California—San Jose—Biography. 5. Mount Pleasant High School (San
Jose, Calif.) 6. San Jose (Calif.)—Social conditions. 7. Educational change—California. 8. California—
Social policy. 9. California—Politics and government—1951– I. Title.
F866.4.P65A3 2010
979.4'053—dc22   2009050136

Printed in the United States of America
Set in Warnock Pro · Designed by Amy Hill

Penguin is committed to publishing works of quality and integrity.
In that spirit, we are proud to offer this book to our readers;
However, the story, the experiences, and the words
are the author's alone.

To my past Mount Pleasant High School students:
You taught me many valuable lessons.

To the school's future students:
All my profits from the sale of this book go to make
Mount Pleasant an ever better place to learn.

Contents

Author's Note

Surprises, I'd argue, stay with you. When I decided to explore a completely different profession, and surround myself with a very unfamiliar community, I encountered lots of surprises. Surprises that crept into my head and heart. Surprises that colored my perspective on kids and society. Surprises about myself. Years later, I haven't forgotten many of the revelations brought about by teaching at a struggling public high school.

I hope this story—a fish-out-of-water tale of a prolific entrepreneur who calls on all of his abilities to try to succeed as a rookie schoolteacher—speaks to you. Maybe you're interested in becoming a teacher, or have always dreamed of volunteering in a classroom full of underprivileged kids, and want to know what you might encounter. Perhaps you're a professional who might gain from the best business practices that I applied to run a classroom. Maybe you're interested in politics and want to know how I'll take the lessons I learned while teaching and apply them directly to reform California's compromised public school system. Or you could be a parent of school-aged children, or someone who's thinking of starting a family. This book is also about returning California's public schools—about returning a *nation's* public schools—to their former greatness. What you hold in your hands addresses our children's future.

I will say, no matter who you are, thank you. Thanks for picking up my book and giving me the opportunity to tell you my tale. Writing it gave me the chance to relive a lot of incredible moments and experiences. When I finally finished assembling all the memories, I felt that the book's messages were upbeat and empowering. I hope my story leaves you feeling similarly satisfied.

A Note Regarding People and Names

This is a work of nonfiction. The events in the book all occurred as they've been characterized. All of the places I describe exist. All of the people in the book are real individuals, and when they're quoted, I re-created actual conversations to the best of my recollections. However, I did not begin my association with Mount Pleasant High School almost eight years ago thinking that I would one day write a book about my experiences. Yet this was a story that I ultimately decided to tell, and there is content within the book that's based on a combination of research and recall. When I made up my mind to write the book, many records from my time spent teaching at Mount Pleasant were unavailable to me.

I changed the names of nearly everyone I came in contact with at Mount Pleasant. I also made occasional and intentional changes to some of the characters' physical attributes, job responsibilities, and histories.

I made these changes for one reason: I wanted to protect the people I was associated with at Mount Pleasant from any embarrassment or unwanted public attention. My fellow teachers, as well as my students, did not think that I would someday write a book about them. Their prior openness with me shouldn't be repaid with unwelcome exposure. As a result, changing characters' identities allowed me more freedom to describe the personalities, emotions, conditions, and events as I truly found them. I believe that the struggles at Mount Pleasant are echoed at other public high schools in California, and across the nation. I can only hope that my chronicling of real emotions and frustrations brings about positive change in the country's education policies.

My business colleagues are identified by their real names. I've also used real names for everyone involved in my year as a White House Fellow.

Everyone in my family is identified by their real names. Even my old golden retriever, Jake.

Acknowledgments

Thanks must begin with the people who helped me turn a barrel of recollections and memorabilia into a wonderful book. Stuart Stevens at the Stevens and Schriefer Group, Peter Matson at Sterling Lord Literistic, Inc., and Adrian Zackheim at Penguin Group's Portfolio head the list. Other key contributors include Joy Tutela at the David Black Literary Agency, as well as Portfolio's Jonah Blumstein and Courtney Young. Special gratitude goes to Andrew Tilin: We couldn't have done this without Andrew's smarts, writing abilities, and hard work.

There were also invaluable contributions from my staff and campaign team, and I'm grateful to Jarrod Agen, Candace Amundson, Jim Bognet, Lanhee Chen, Jesse Huff, Audrey Perry, and Kevin Spillane. Then there's the incomparable Robert Molnar, who replies to my queries as fast as I can hit the SEND button.

Joe Anastasi, Sandy Bails, Anna Graham, Kate Hartley, Jeff Kunkel, Ron Parker, Jim Richardson, and Sally Small all provided great feedback on the manuscript, often chapter by chapter. Donna Terman gets special thanks—an MVP reader who provided me with tremendous background knowledge, extensive comments, and ample encouragement. You were right from the start, Donna. I had to roll up my sleeves and get into a classroom.

Chris Lockard, Fred Lowell, and Cydney Tune provided confidence-inspiring counsel. Meanwhile Vanessa Barth, Alison Biggar, Laura Hohnhold, and Bob Ickes crossed every *t* when it came to tasks like transcription, editing, and checking facts.

I can't say enough about the associates, friends, and family who helped jog my memory and then some. I thought I had good tales to tell until I heard from Margaret Berry, Neilson Buchanan, Luis Buhler, Bena Fisher, Grettel Castro-Stanley, Beth Cooper, Reed Hastings, Irwin Jacobs, Norm Krasner, Jeff Lefkowitz, Mike Lynn, Ken Oshman, Howard Poizner, Don Shalvey, Kevin Smith, Peter Thorp, Scott Wallace, Don and Sylvie Way, Jocelyn White, Caprice Young, and Howard Zucker. You all know me maybe a little *too* well.

Without the principal, teachers, and staff of Mount Pleasant High School there would be no book. Thank you a million times over for your openness, patience, intelligence, and dedication. Don't let anyone tell you differently: You do the world's most important work. The future is in your hands.

As for *my* future, I am nothing without my family. To the Lucias: I deeply appreciate your constant support, and your enormous appetite for stress-busting card games. And to my wife, Carol, and daughter, Rebecca: I love you both. Keep the life lessons coming.

Mount Pleasant

Why Are You Here?

One September day in 2002, I drove from my home in North-ern California's wooded hills into the heart of a city. I came to do a good deed. Walking into a school administrative building, I found a receptionist and asked her if I could volunteer.

"I'm really interested in teaching," I said, opening my palms to help explain myself. "You know, in a classroom."

The secretary seemed bewildered. She said nothing. Instead she excused herself and returned with another woman. Dark-haired, com-pact, with the furrowed brow of a guard dog, the woman identified herself as a personnel manager.

"Hello. I understand you have a request," she said, her arms crossed. "Now, what is it that you want? Why are you here?"

The reply that first came to mind: I want to help people. I mean, I want to help people in a way that I haven't before. Up to now, my success as an entrepreneur, and my egg-headed habits, have brought those

1

around me considerable wealth and other benefits, too—my young daughter, for one, gets real satisfaction out of calling me a geek. I also wanted to say to the woman that I've had a passion for learning ever since I was a kid, and that I wanted to share my love of learning with others. I was in that building, I rather innocently thought, so that I could apply my business smarts and problem-solving skills, along with my enthusiasm for schooling, to the public education system. And what better place for me to help than in the neglected schools near where I lived? Schools in the same Silicon Valley where I'd made my fortune?

Admittedly, I still had plenty to learn about education. But, as crazy as it sounds, my thread of logic made sense to me, because I've accomplished much of what I've ever set out to do. I thought that if I were given the chance and a little time, I could have a positive impact on a classroom. I thought I could somehow pitch in.

"Well, my name is Steve Poizner. I want to volunteer," I explained. "To teach. I don't want to get paid."

The woman narrowed her eyes. We were, after all, in the administrative headquarters for the challenged East Side Union High School District, located in San Jose, California. Its collection of schools host an overwhelming number of underprivileged students. Dropout rates hover around 7 percent (approaching twice the national average), and most graduates don't go on to four-year colleges. East Side schools have seen bloodshed on campus, and students on the school's playing fields hear gunshots from surrounding neighborhoods.

The woman also didn't know me from Adam. Here I was, in khakis, a pressed shirt, and loafers, looking just like the forty-five-year-old trim and graying engineer that I was. But she could have easily thought I was some preppy weirdo. Would anyone with any real sense be so naïve as to think that he could walk into the offices of a huge public school district and grab a teaching job?

But she didn't call security. She played along.

"Mr., uh," she continued.

"Poizner," I offered.

"Mr. Poizner," she said. "Tell me what qualifies you to be in the classroom."

I launched into a spiel that used to work beautifully in executives' offices.

"I graduated top of my class in electrical engineering at the University of Texas, got an MBA with honors from Stanford, and then spent twenty years starting and running successful tech companies in Silicon Valley," I said. "I also worked in the White House—in the National Security Council."

She nodded before shaking her head.

"Mr. Poizner, nothing you've described qualifies you to be in the classroom," she said. "Thank you for your interest." Then she walked away.

Not long before, I'd quit a big corporate job because I had visions of helping my adopted, longtime home state. Yet my new odyssey's first indelible image was of a gruff middle manager showing me her back.

Truthfully, the bureaucrat wasn't alone in telling me to stay away. My friends repeatedly said there were plenty of other ways to help. Education veterans warned me that the classrooms inside a struggling public school bore zero resemblance to, say, my then eleven-year-old daughter's buoyant private-school surroundings. My wife Carol worried about my safety, and for good reason. I didn't know the first thing about the rough neighborhoods that host many of San Jose's compromised public schools.

Nonetheless, as I walked out into the hazy sunshine of that Northern California day, I resolved not to give up. That wouldn't be me—

stubborn, solution-obsessed me. But what I couldn't know in that moment was how naïve I really was. Public school classrooms can be dispiriting. Some of the school buildings are literally coming apart. Teachers are frequently wary of newcomers spouting off suggestions. And worst of all, the toughest students range from indifferent to downright scary. During the year that I ended up immersing myself in a troubled public high school, I harnessed all of my expertise as a seasoned business leader to create success in the classroom. Sometimes I had the answers. Often I came to ask myself one question: What exactly *are* you doing here?

As it turns out, I was receiving one hell of an education.

CHAPTER 1

Entrepreneur or Bust

I
t's funny how two decades of hard-won career experience can,
all at once, leave you both wise and remarkably innocent. During
my days as an entrepreneur, I had no reason to explore Silicon
Valley. If I had, maybe I would have realized it resembles an enormous
microchip. Neighborhoods and shopping areas, like components set
on a miniature piece of silicon substrate, stake out their territory. The
surroundings are colorful. But the landscape, whether you're talking
about an integrated circuit or the Valley, can be sorted into two cate-
gories: places full of energy, activity, and commerce, and, well, everything else. There are walls between these two areas, even though they're
difficult or impossible to see. But make no mistake: They're walls.

One day in 1983, my boss reminded me how privileged life was on
the dynamic side of the walls. I was just a kid, twenty-six, wearing a
suit that hung off me as well as the oversized glasses of your classic
cube-dwelling geek.

"You want to do *what*?" he said, running a hand through his surfer mane. He defined prosperity in the Valley. He was tall and athletic, had an office with a view, and PARTNER printed on his business cards. "You don't want to do that," he added.

I swiped my mop of brown hair over in a way that kept my part straight.

"You're in a really good spot here," he continued. "Why turn your back on it?"

It was a legitimate question. I was only three years out of business school and into this job. A job I was lucky to have, too—as a junior consultant at the top-notch Boston Consulting Group. I'd already worked with some of BCG's Fortune 500 clients. I was making good money. Everywhere I looked there were smarts and wealth. What else could a career-minded kid want?

"Now is also a great time to be an entrepreneur," I found myself saying, pushing my glasses back up onto the bridge of my nose. "I thought I'd launch my own business."

Like so many before me, I'd come west with visions. I sympathized with all the other California dreamers: the nineteenth-century pioneers clawing for gold; the girl next door, who had hopes for screen stardom and the phone number of some Hollywood agent; the farmers who migrated to the Central Valley to grow crops that would feed the country.

I aspired to a California fantasy more in step with the pocket-protector set. Coming from Houston and a low-key but education-minded family, I'd thought about inventing things ever since I was a kid who had made the local Radio Shack his second home. In college, I had believed that engineering and electronics were full of possibilities—possibilities that, to my mind, were eclipsed only by the idea of creating entire companies that could put high-tech inventions into the hands of many, many people. I had migrated to Northern California for business school, deciding against pursuing a Harvard MBA in the process. Stanford, after all, was in the Silicon Valley.

My boss cupped his clean-shaven chin in his hand. He had always been fair with me, and even-keeled. But wrinkles of irritation were forming like so many fault lines on his forehead. Junior staffers didn't regularly walk out on Boston Consulting. They didn't leave BCG's prestige behind.

He took a big breath.

"You're doing good work for us, Steve," he said, clasping his hands. "Starting your own business is incredibly risky. The fall from grace can be abrupt and sobering."

But tech industry icons were already dancing in my head. My heroes were innovators like Bill Gates and Steve Jobs. Personal computers were landing on desks across America at a rapid clip. To me, the work involving those men and machines was a lot more compelling than business consulting. I was too inexperienced to feel anxious about risk and the overwhelming number of start-up companies that fail. All I felt was excitement.

And the walls? What did I know back then of walls? I was young, and determined to carve out my spot in the Valley. I had no sense of the lesser life, including the anger and disappointment that thrives on the other side of any walls. I had no clue that the challenges someday posed to me by a bunch of wayward kids, and a down-on-its-luck school only a few miles from my boss's perch, would humble me in a way that no venture capitalist or bloodthirsty technology company ever could.

"I appreciate your kind words. And all the chances," is what I think came out of my mouth next. My mind was already out the door. "I'm moving on," I added.

The fact that my boss didn't want to start on the ground floor with another kid fresh out of school probably had everything to do with what happened next. His warning about falling from grace and the threat of learning about life on the other side of the wall were all about keeping my desk occupied. Not about me in particular. Or was I mistaken? I wouldn't fully appreciate his feedback—his rather thunderous response—for another twenty years.

He lost it. "You don't know what you're giving up!" he said loudly, the veins in his neck bulging. "You don't know what's out there!"

Within weeks, I launched a business with two other guys out of a cramped Santa Clara town house. We were living the clichéd Silicon Valley start-up existence: Work out of a bedroom, eat pizza in front of our computers, sleep on couches, and work some more. The town house was on a well-worn nine-hole golf course. But I never swung a club. I didn't care. I was in my element, honing a vision, crunching numbers, and building a business plan. I had eyes only for becoming one of the entrepreneurial elite.

When you haven't experienced much in the way of failure, every idea seems solid. After leaving Boston Consulting Group, I thought my concept for a business was dead-on. It was 1983; consumers were marveling at the personal computer's monochromatic screen and just figuring out how to send word-processing documents to a printer. Based on work I had been doing at BCG, I figured consumers would soon be hungering for digital maps.

I should say that was my hunch. There were plenty of people who could not wrap their heads around the concept. A digital what? What's "digital"?

I didn't want to sell any old digital maps, either. Not the kind that we use every day today, for finding the nearest ATM or movie theater. My worldview was a lot narrower. I wanted to capitalize on what I saw as an emerging market in "geographic information systems."

I'll explain: At Boston Consulting Group I'd become the go-to guy for providing large clients with a new service that used mapping information to help them identify what made their companies' outlets more or less successful. Big corporations like Bank of America would give me the addresses of a few of their branches, and other information such as square footage and revenues. Then I'd plug in variables, like population density around the business, location of the closest competition, and a demographic breakdown of the surrounding neighborhoods. These numbers would run through a set of mathematical formulas to determine the five or so factors that were most influential in terms of the locations' performances. The digital maps turned spreadsheet-style statistics into more digestible information.

This was not sexy. Still, huge corporations with hundreds of storefronts used the analysis to expand or contract their businesses.

Because this tool at BCG was wrapped up with other services for the company's clients, it came at a steep price. My idea was to provide much of the same highbrow wisdom in a software package for personal computers. I'd sell it in stores for around $500. I dubbed my new company Strategic Mapping, and by 1985 we had about fifty employees and a software product called Atlas.

Developing product, however, wasn't the same as creating a company. Get hired at a company and you learn how to do a job, or at least the minimum required to keep it. But start a company, especially when you're young and green, and you learn how to do every job. Strategic Mapping began with my savings and a small-business loan, and there were days when I was chief shrink-wrapper, enveloping our products in plastic. I also assembled binders, rearranged workspaces, and helped the UPS man with boxes.

I learned a few things about management, too. My hiring processes were textbook—check references, look at past performance, be mindful of personality and team chemistry. But process was the problem. Stanford MBA or no, I wasn't yet mature enough to have a reliable sixth sense about people.

I put good hires into ill-suited positions and let some of the wrong people through the door. One time I was completely won over by a job candidate with twenty years' experience. I was convinced that he was going to make a fantastic vice president of sales.

A few weeks after I hired him, I wondered why it was taking him so long to mix with our salespeople in the field. I kept calling his office. "How's it going?" I'd ask. "Got everything you need?"

I was finding that I had little patience for people who couldn't keep up with my pace.

One day I walked into his office to give him a prod, and discovered why he was so slow. He'd been busy decorating his space with mahogany furniture and hanging framed diplomas on the walls. I reminded him that we were a start-up and that our mission was to conquer the world, or at least one software shelf at national computer stores. My office had a ten-dollar Renoir print on the wall and it hung crooked. The VP didn't have enough fire in his belly. He was gone within a year.

Back then the geographic information systems market was crowded. We scrounged for every sale. We worked with unlikely clients, like police departments wanting to map out patrol routes. Honda used our software to help the company decide where to open motorcycle dealerships. Word around the office of a $10,000 sales deal called for high fives. But on a chilly February 1990 day—some seven years into Strategic Mapping's existence—we hit $10 million in annual sales. The business milestone was cause for a celebration of sorts, as I promptly kept a commitment to my employees by swimming in the fountain in front of our headquarters, which were then in Santa Clara. In another five years we'd sell the company for about $30 million.

The transaction, which happened in 1995, hardly made me a master of the universe—I feel like Microsoft grosses that kind of money in mere hours. But I'd gone from zero to president to a marketer of real products to sale of the company, a Silicon Valley rite of passage. I was in the right place, and with my tribe of like-minded entrepreneurs, whose lives revolved around daring business moves and trying to solve the world's problems. Our world's problems, I should say, as seen from behind the walls.

"You need some sun," Carol said to me one day shortly after we'd sold Strategic Mapping. I was creeping up on forty, and gray had begun to appear in my hair. I took karate, but still looked more like Rick Moranis than Bruce Lee. And thanks to work, I'd missed a lot of early moments with our then four-year-old daughter, Rebecca.

One day, we all escaped to the ballpark. I hadn't seen the San Francisco Giants play in ages. Enjoying a blessedly windless afternoon at Candlestick, I had a rare moment to reflect on something other than business. Carol was the one who urged me to eat somewhere besides my desk, picked up the clothes that I absentmindedly dropped on the floor every night, and believed me when I walked away from that job at BCG on the assurance that there were greener pastures.

She and I had essentially met on a baseball diamond. Back in 1980, as members of the networking-oriented Palo Alto Junior

Chamber (Jaycees) organization, we were a couple of twentysome-
thing kids who enjoyed joking together at occasional Jaycees softball
games. Carol was working for AT&T and I was frequently arriving
late to the social gatherings after spending long days at Boston Consulting.

We soon discovered that we were drawn to each other: We both
sipped on the beer that our peers sometimes drank in copious amounts,
and yet still managed to keep up with everyone else's alcohol-fueled
goofiness. I valued Carol's love of family and friends, and she appreciated that I was such a hard worker.

I should say she appreciated and tolerated my passion for work.
Who else would go out a second time with a man so exhausted by
his job that he fell asleep on her shoulder—while watching *A Chorus
Line*—on their first date? Carol's big brown eyes always communi-
cated warmth and kindness, and her thick, dark hair hinted at her
mostly Italian heritage. When I finally proposed to Carol in 1986 she
looked beautiful, and offered a girlish grin and a "yes," despite my in-
home, candlelight dinner featuring the only foods I knew how to
prepare: Swanson chicken potpie and a Sara Lee frozen strawberry
cheesecake.

I remember gulping a lot before popping the question. Pitching
potential investors for start-up money had been easy by comparison.

Even before my first company's sale was final, I was thinking about
the next move, addicted to what Strategic Mapping had given me.
Money was part of it, although financially speaking, as long as I didn't
start buying swaths of land or expensive art, selling the company had
given me a bit of a cash cushion. What I really loved was creating and
establishing a business, not unlike the way a conductor gathers and

knits together an orchestra. I had experienced the entrepreneurial equivalent of clashing cymbals, and I wanted to hear that sound again.

I thought there might be a new business idea related to Strategic Mapping that involved some *Jetsons*-type technology. I thought the new endeavor could have a much greater impact than my first company, which of course was the standard aspirational mind-set in the Silicon Valley.

Why would I be different? I had never been reluctant to dream big. One time I'd been put in charge of finding speakers for a decidedly low-key gathering, and I invited former President Jimmy Carter, former Canadian Prime Minister Pierre Trudeau, and former Chief Justice Warren Burger. They all said they were busy, and we ended up listening to a football coach. But if I had to do it all over I would aim very high again.

The new technology had to do with electronic navigation. Some of Strategic Mapping's clients were using our software in concert with brand-new, portable navigation devices that received their pinpoint information from a network of twenty-four U.S. satellites.

The collection of satellites, called the Global Positioning System and built by the Department of Defense, orbits the earth and beams radio waves that deliver location-oriented data back down to individual receiving units.

By the mid-1990s GPS data had been largely declassified. There was a growing consumer market for GPS receivers in cars and boats. Backpackers and traveling businessmen also wanted them. Personally, I noticed that some of the utility companies that were Strategic Mapping customers were also using GPS information to identify the locations of their equipment in the field. My clients were then entering that data into Atlas mapping software.

Shortly before we sold Strategic Mapping, I saw a sobering TV news story that made me think there was more potential for this GPS wizardry. It reported that a quadriplegic in the Midwest had suffered a heart attack while driving. His van had come to a halt atop a set of railroad tracks.

Events then unfolded with agonizing predictability. The handicapped driver couldn't get out of his van. He called 911, but he knew only that he was on a train track . . . somewhere. The dispatcher couldn't locate the caller. A train appeared on the horizon.

It got me thinking: What if GPS—or something like it—could somehow be employed as a tracking technology? Maybe it could locate people, or cars. I wondered if it could prevent tragedies, like when people get trapped, lost, or injured. Or when a van stalls in front of a speeding train.

Within months of selling Strategic Mapping, Carol and some other family members were singing "Happy Birthday" to me inside a mostly empty workspace on San Jose's Moorpark Avenue. I'd rented the office for my new company, SnapTrack. The lyrics echoed through the place, and the chocolate cake, marking my thirty-ninth year, was set down on a card table that doubled as the office conference table. At the time, the company employed about four people. I wasn't even sure what SnapTrack would make.

Despite my degree in electrical engineering, someone else would have to connect the technological dots for the company. I didn't have the right skill set, and I hoped to be busy running a business. Fortunately, Silicon Valley was rich in smart, hardworking engineers, and a quirky guy named Norm Krasner intrigued me. With engineering degrees from Stanford and MIT, a passion for a sophisticated numerical computing language called MATLAB, and extensive experience as a signal-processing contractor for the defense industry, the fifty-year-old Krasner was among the brainiest of the brainy.

"We'd consider GPS and terrestrial triangulation among our options," he said in our initial interview, and I didn't know exactly what he was suggesting. Krasner also rubbed his high-gloss forehead a lot, which seemed to precipitate more comments about scientific theories and math equations. Just short of being too preoccupied to shake my hand, he agreed to work on my team. Ultimately SnapTrack's core decision-making group would grow to about a dozen key people addressing responsibilities that included engineering, marketing, legal issues, software, and product design.

But it was Krasner's intelligence, research, and determination that helped motivate us through SnapTrack's initial, uncertain months. When you're vague about the product you're creating, or the technology behind it, the life of an entrepreneur can be lonely. Making matters worse, if you can't tell potential investors exactly what it is you're building, they're slow to reach for their checkbooks. I soon became very familiar with Moorpark Avenue's sidewalks. I'd take breaks from the office and get lost in my thoughts while pacing the neighborhood concrete. During those breathers, I seldom heard the sound of Moorpark's ever-present traffic.

The company's few other engineers and I wondered if GPS really was an option. The technology is fantastic, but has an Achilles' heel: By the time GPS signals reach earth, they're weak. For a car stereo, a weak radio signal is a staticky annoyance. But a severely weakened GPS signal is useless. When I started SnapTrack, virtually every GPS device available required an unimpeded view of the sky to work. Everyone presumed that GPS technology could never work inside a building, or under leafy trees in a park.

Which made Krasner's epiphany—at least the one he had on a rainy winter day in early 1996—all the more unbelievable.

"Steve!" he said, hurrying into my office, rubbing his forehead, his shirt half untucked. "Let's incorporate GPS into cell phones! We can find the location of every single cell phone!"

Krasner explained how cell phones and existing cell phone networks were, with some modifications, uniquely equipped to receive and interpret weakened GPS signals. SnapTrack could develop those modifications and help deliver reliable location data wherever one of these next-generation cell phones worked. His discovery had the chance of becoming a real breakthrough, with potentially enormous market appeal. Hundreds of millions of mobile phones were sold each year.

Armed with a concrete idea, my job was fun again. Soon a big door cracked open for SnapTrack: Krasner and I got the chance to present our preliminary findings and nascent technology to experts at the federal government's Defense Advanced Research Projects Agency, or DARPA, in Arlington, Virginia. We thought we might get grant money, and credibility, too—DARPA performs research and design for the Department of Defense. The agency invented the Internet.

But after flying cross-country for the meeting, we were barely warmed up inside DARPA's stark offices before a communications technology guru shook his head.

"I've considered your idea before," the man said. "I don't need to hear any more."

Krasner was stunned. "What are you talking about?" he asked, adding that we were already applying for patents. "This has never been done."

Inexplicably, the engineer soon got up and left the room. Krasner and I looked at each other. What had just happened? Many of our claims were still on paper, but that's exactly why we'd come three thousand miles: to take the next step. We thought a technology that could potentially track soldiers' locations was a slam dunk. But within an hour of arriving, we were returning our visitor's badges and heading to the door.

The response was equally dubious back in Northern California. People were stunned at our claims, as if we were members of the Flat Earth Society. Engineers called us crazy: GPS, they repeated to us ad nauseam, could not work inside buildings.

I caught myself wondering if the doubters were right, and if I'd earned some kind of unprecedented title as an entrepreneur: The Man Who Dreamed Too Big. Was that even possible in the Silicon Valley?

SnapTrack was fortunate to have a couple of Valley veterans on its side. Attorney Craig Johnson pushed us to keep applying for patents. And Ken Oshman, a highly respected Valley engineer and entrepreneur, gave us approximately one million dollars in seed money and joined our company's board of directors. Nonetheless, Oshman seemed more intrigued than convinced by our pitch. We were just a tiny business, he pointed out, with an iffy technology. He also knew that the mobile phone industry was packed with huge, well-funded companies, and controlled by myriad federal regulations. Maybe, Oshman added, the people we had encountered thought that SnapTrack's technology might even someday work, but that the company could never pull off the development. We could get pushed aside by a much bigger player.

"I don't know," he said, leaning back in his office chair with a sardonic smile. "Seems like a crapshoot to me." But we were willing to endure Oshman's hesitation, especially when it came combined with his investment.

I was determined to make SnapTrack a go. Still believing the military could help us showcase our technology, I inquired at the Pentagon and anywhere else people in uniform might listen. One day in 1996 the navy threw the company what I considered to be a lifeline. A San Diego–based military program asked us to help keep tabs on its dolphins.

The navy trains dolphins for combat purposes such as sea-mine detection and identifying enemy swimmers. What it sought was a system that could track each of its approximately seventy dorsal-finned recruits, because every so often one would swim off and never return. Krasner and I admitted to each other that this was a pretty weird opportunity. What next? SnapTrack for dogs, featuring a two-for-one locator/flea collar? But the navy offered to pay us, and we'd also get the opportunity to further test our technology in the field.

SnapTrack's board of directors was emphatic in its response.

"Are you nuts?" Oshman said one day at our Moorpark offices. "What's the size of that market? Three marine mammals? Plus you'll have to deal with all sorts of red tape. Stay focused."

That wasn't what I wanted to hear. Finally we hadn't been called crackpots, and now we had to turn down a potential customer.

But I came around to Oshman's line of logic. One of the hallmarks of a successful, big-thinking entrepreneur is his or her ability to ignore the noise that can cause a young company to stray from its mission. Apple stuck with Mac. Intel stuck with chips. SnapTrack had to be about locating mobile phones, not dolphins.

I poured my resources into hiring more staff. I wanted to build relationships with cell phone manufacturers, related electronics businesses, mobile-phone-service providers, and the Federal Communications Commission.

Why did SnapTrack want to make friends at the FCC? Because 1996 was also the year when the Federal Communications Commission originally mandated that all mobile phones would have to be locatable by 911 operators—via some type of innovation—by 2001. That ruling, however, wasn't initially beneficial to us at SnapTrack. Quite the opposite: The original FCC mandate called for a technology that would make all new and existing phones locatable. SnapTrack's technology couldn't be retrofitted into mobile phones currently in use. We wanted to convince the FCC to broaden its decree in such a way that our product would be considered viable. Making the challenge even more difficult, the commission's mandate increased the potential for other companies to jump into the market. Indeed, huge, established businesses ultimately joined the race.

But even before the competition heated up, we felt like SnapTrack had some distinct advantages. Krasner and the company's other engineers could not only prove that our technology worked. They knew that SnapTrack's GPS-based technology was far more precise than another concept that had been proposed: locator technology that used cell phone towers, not satellites. Such "terrestrial" technology was accurate only within dozens, if not hundreds, of yards, while SnapTrack's GPS-oriented technology was accurate within feet. The terrestrial technology also required that modifications be made to literally every cell tower. SnapTrack's technology didn't require such modifications. While we kept working the FCC, we also refined our invention, and applied for dozens of key patents related to GPS-sensing technology embedded in mobile phones.

We also gained support from the cell phone industry. By mid-1997 our engineers had worked in conjunction with many of the industry's big hitters, including Sprint, Verizon, Texas Instruments, Samsung, Motorola, and LG. Such companies, in fact, established a consortium to work together with our technology. They were drawn to SnapTrack in part because of its promise to deliver both superior performance and value. Among other things, the consortium helped us validate our technology with third-party testing, and assisted us in decreasing the size of our parts. For example, Motorola helped reduce our antenna technology until it was virtually invisible to the user.

Sure enough, within a year, the SnapTrack locator technology that would ultimately have to be shoehorned into a mobile phone shrank from something that rested on a hand truck to something that fit inside a container the size of a cigarette box. The miniaturization got the attention of a marine colonel at the Pentagon, who was intrigued by SnapTrack's work but unconvinced that it performed as advertised. In 1998 he challenged the company to a duel.

One day the colonel met me and some SnapTrack engineers in a small downtown San Francisco work space. The colonel was a no-nonsense man who appeared to be in his fifties, and had thick eyebrows and a booming, Patton-type voice. He'd brought along a small entourage and a lot of equipment.

"I've been working on this location technology for years," he said, helping one of his soldiers strap on a huge backpack stuffed with electronics and topped by a tall whip antenna. Then the colonel pointed to the load. "Bet my stuff is better than yours," he added.

Team SnapTrack entered one of our doughy tech geeks into the competition. He was dwarfed by the muscular, backpack-carrying marine.

Our guy put SnapTrack's locator gizmo, which was taped to a cell phone, in his shirt pocket. Then the two of them walked out into the breezy San Francisco afternoon, and we followed their progress on a computer. The men appeared as individual blipping dots moving across a map of the area.

For a time they moved together. Then the dot representing the SnapTrack engineer inexplicably stopped, while the marine's dot kept going. I turned away from the monitor. Was I losing the highest-stakes video game of my life?

The colonel leaned toward the screen for a closer look. "Is there a problem here?" he purred, grinning and assuming that our technology was fizzling. The military man was going to show a bunch of Silicon Valley dweebs who was boss!

But only our engineer had faltered. While the super-fit marine powered over San Francisco's hills, my employee ran out of gas and stopped at a Starbucks. SnapTrack's streamlined equipment had worked perfectly. When our man returned from the field, I didn't know whether to punch or hug him.

Nailing that trial was huge. The colonel was gracious in admitting to the benefits of our much more compact technology and wrote a glowing report about our company. The endorsement helped bring us a lot of opportunity. SnapTrack was invited to do more testing with industry-related companies around the world, and by late 1998 we convinced the FCC that its mandate needed to accommodate our technology. SnapTrack's innovation was precise and could be implemented without adding much cost to a phone—or to a phone company. Plus consumers are constantly buying new mobile phones. Ultimately, the FCC tweaked its ruling in such a way that we could become a leading player in mobile-phone locator technology.

Getting past huge engineering, government, and market challenges, SnapTrack's office phones began ringing off the hook. Everyone wanted to invest in us, and by the fall of 1999 we were on the verge of raising millions of dollars courtesy of top Silicon Valley venture capitalists and mobile-phone industry companies from as far off as Japan. The next step, I thought, was taking SnapTrack public.

Then I had a curious phone conversation. It was with Jeff Jacobs, who worked under his father, Irwin, who headed San Diego–based Qualcomm. Qualcomm is a leading chip maker in the cell phone industry, and back in 1999 was already a $4 billion company. I'd hoped that Qualcomm would license our technology, but negotiations had stalled for years. I figured that what Qualcomm really wanted was to devise a locator technology of its own, which could have crushed us.

Hoping for a friendlier solution, I wondered over the phone if Jacobs wanted to invest in my company now. I said that SnapTrack's star was rising fast, and reminded him that the FCC's deadline for placing locator technology into cell phones was looming. In the back of my mind, I was banking on SnapTrack's extensive portfolio of sought after patents. At some point, I'd hoped, Qualcomm would have to do business with us.

Much to my surprise, Jacobs was interested. But he wanted to invest a disproportionately large amount—about $10 million. That would have given Qualcomm enough investor power to steer Snap-Track's fate.

"Either make a smaller investment or a much larger one, Jeff," I said. Then I half-joked: "You could buy the whole company."

"Let's talk about that second option," he said, almost as if on cue.

I wasn't expecting that. SnapTrack was hot and probably valued at hundreds of millions of dollars. I rounded up.

"We'll have to start at one billion dollars," I said.

"I'll call you back in ten minutes," he replied.

I don't know if I even said good-bye. Ten minutes later the phone rang. It was Jacobs. I wondered if he could hear my heart pounding.

"Okay," he said. "A billion."

Even for a math dork like me, the figure was almost unimaginable.

Shortly after that conversation, I drove home. I was stunned.

"Are you all right?" Carol asked.

"You won't believe what happened today," I said.

.   .   .

Right in the heart of the Valley, Menlo Park's Dutch Goose restaurant specializes in power lunches for the area's nouveau riche. The rustic eatery serves food fast—all the better for the hard-driving boss who wants to get back to his desk. The house specialty is spicy deviled eggs; I'm a cheeseburger man myself.

"With fries," I ordered. "And a Coke."

It was a winter day in early 2001, and I was out of the office for a brief lunch break with three other Valley execs. I was proud to think that I belonged at the table. SnapTrack was sold to Qualcomm in January 2000 for $1 billion. The sale didn't make me a billionaire, but it brought me way more money than I thought I'd ever see. The transaction made a lot of the other sixty-five former employees at SnapTrack rich, too: From the receptionist on up, everyone's shares in the company were worth $1 million or more.

Nonetheless, most former SnapTrackers, including Krasner and me, had stuck with Qualcomm since the purchase. We'd worked out of a Silicon Valley office of the company, helping with the merger and then some. I had a reasonable shot at becoming Qualcomm senior management.

But after spending twenty years working my way to the top, I arrived at these power lunches only to find the shine coming off the Valley's signature high-stakes forms of business. The executives spent as much time complaining as they did brainstorming, and often mentioned looking outside the Valley for new ventures.

The complaints weren't all attributable to the infamous bursting of the dot-com bubble, either. That decline began abruptly in early 2000 and was a result, among other things, of many nascent Internet-related companies going bust because they weren't profitable and couldn't sustain the losses brought on by a rapidly receding stock market.

The problems being aired to me were more systemic. California was making it harder for someone to launch and run a business. Workers' compensation costs were rising, taxes were high, regulations were tightening, and the public education system continued its downward spiral. Add to that the Bay Area's notoriously steep housing costs, and was it any wonder why my peers believed that fewer people were willing to come west and roll the dice?

Silicon Valley was hardly going to fold in on itself. It still hosted many aspiring entrepreneurs with great ideas, and the Golden State's scenery and sunshine would undoubtedly always pull in plenty of people.

But I understood my buddies' lack of ease, and I was agitated, too— although for slightly different reasons. The transition at work had gone well. All of Qualcomm's top men—Irwin and Jeff Jacobs, as well as Jeff's brother Paul—were happy with their purchase, and Qualcomm would ultimately weave SnapTrack's technology into its electronics, and into hundreds of millions of mobile phones. SnapTrack's innovation would end up saving many lives.

Still, I didn't want to stick around. I'd done the exciting work. I had heard the cymbals clash. I wasn't interested in being a cog in any large company—even a world-beating organization like Qualcomm.

But I couldn't imagine retiring, either. Despite my sudden wealth, a life of jet-shares, Lamborghinis, and McMansion acquisitions wasn't an option. I've never been into stuff, which occasionally drives Carol crazy: what she wouldn't do to get me interested in buying furniture, redoing a kitchen, or dressing in something other than blue jeans or entrepreneur khaki. And while I knew I wanted to give away some money, I didn't want to spend my days as a philanthropist, either. I needed more substance.

I spent some of my time away from the office considering options.

I met with managers of gigantic Silicon Valley charity foundations. But I was ambivalent about the prospect of giving away other people's money, too. I also received multiple offers from venture capitalists and CEOs to lead fledgling companies in need of seasoned management, and that was tempting. At forty-four, there was no question that I still wanted to tackle huge challenges.

In fact, it was my near-perverse desire for challenge that had me, for the first time since I'd become an entrepreneur, wondering what lurks outside the world of start-ups. I thought about my peers' multiple complaints regarding the state of California. Government reform? Health care? Public education? Those were some big, juicy problems.

One day during my search, I came across an intriguing front-page story in *The Wall Street Journal*. It was about a California school superintendent intent on shaking up the state's lackluster and calcified kindergarten-through-twelfth-grade education system. The article featured words like *entrepreneur, business plans,* and *deliverables.* That's my kind of talk, I thought, and I pondered the notion of putting my worker-bee sensibilities to use outside the world of high technology. "There's risk: What happens if you fail?" the superintendent was quoted as saying in the story. "What happens if you succeed?"

After reading that story, I also thought back on my own childhood education experiences. They'd been fantastic. My mother, a teacher and lifelong student herself, taught her four children to seek satisfaction in their studies. Growing up, my house was quiet almost every afternoon, as the Poizner family hit the books. In school as a kid, I'd had the chance to build a laser from scratch, and was never discouraged when I zoomed through high school a year early. Then, while enjoying every minute of college, I became a nationally recognized engineering student. Plus the entire school experience—which was an entirely *public school* experience—prepared me for nothing less than business school at Stanford.

Reflecting on how much education had meant to me, and how the education field could involve invention and risk, I got that same tingly feeling I'd had about twenty years earlier, when I left Boston Consulting Group to become an entrepreneur.

One morning in the spring of 2001, I sat down in Irwin Jacobs's San Diego office. I remember that it had an incredible view. At the time, Irwin was Qualcomm's CEO, and definitely part of the tech-geek fraternity: He had big glasses, a wall dedicated to his company's many patents, and an old watch that he refused to surrender because it still kept time. Money had never been the prime motivator for him, either.

"I'd like to move on, Irwin," I said, leaning forward in my seat. "Try something new."

"Like what?" he said, standing beside his desk and putting his hands in his pants pockets. "Another company? Some new innovation?"

"No. This is completely different work. It's not related to Silicon Valley business," I said, crossing my arms.

"You know, all I ever hear these days is that California is a big mess. That you can just see the train wreck coming," I added. "I thought maybe I have the skills to help do something about it."

"Like," he said, "government work?"

"Sort of, yeah," I replied. "Public service. At some point I want to try to help fix California's schools."

"Well that's admirable," he said with a nod. "I'm all for people getting involved. As in, you want to work in a school? Teach?"

I nodded.

He pulled his hands free of his pockets and put them behind his head. "Do you have any idea what you're getting into?"

It was the same line I'd heard many, many years earlier. But Jacobs, unlike my boss back at BCG, was way too much of a gentleman to yell. He wasn't going to tell me that I was sheltered, and that the world I knew was quite small, and sealed as tight as a clean room. Even though he would have been speaking the truth.

Instead Jacobs listened as I offered my resignation. Then he wished me good luck.

CHAPTER 2

A Foot in the Classroom Door

Nearly eighteen months later, I struck out with that unimpressed San Jose school administrator. Watching her recede into the depths of the East Side Union High School District's offices, I was sure she had made a mistake. I could contribute to a classroom. Couldn't I?

I knew a lot about business, economics, marketing—valuable subjects for aspiring high school students. I bet I could hold my own in front of a class, too. I'd managed lots of employees. Would I ever encounter anyone more idiosyncratic than Krasner, or more fickle than a bunch of other Valley geniuses? Plus I hadn't exactly spent the last year and a half relaxing. Instead I'd been researching the issues plaguing California's public schools and getting to know some really inspired people who were advocating for change in education. I had also received great lessons in leadership as a White House Fellow in Washington,

D.C. I thought all this would serve me well in the classroom. If I could just get into one.

I drove home from San Jose on that September day in 2002 and sat down at my desk. Even as a kid, I'd been tenacious; I once bugged my mom relentlessly until she let me play a musical instrument. I'm still not sure, however, that flutophone lessons counted as a real victory.

Almost reflexively, I picked up the phone. I thought that I'd get around the school district headquarters' bureaucrats by appealing directly to school principals.

"Hi, this is Steve Poizner," I said while leaving a voice mail message for one of the principals. "I'm a veteran Silicon Valley entrepreneur interested in sharing my knowledge in a high school classroom. I'm hoping to teach or assist in any capacity. I'd enjoy speaking with you about possible opportunities." I left my telephone number and hung up.

Then I made another call, and another. I phoned East Side's Andrew P. Hill High School. James Lick. Yerba Buena. Piedmont Hills. Silver Creek. I left voice mails at all of those schools, positive that a teacher was needed somewhere in the twenty-thousand-student district. I expected a few calls back.

But my phone didn't ring. An hour went by, and nothing. Responses seldom take that long in the highly caffeinated Valley. By the next afternoon, still nothing.

"You'd think somebody would respond," I said to Carol from my desk. I couldn't see her but figured she was within earshot. "All I ever hear is that these schools could use more resources."

I pushed against the floor with my feet and tilted the chair onto its back legs. Then I let the chair come down to rest with a slight thump every time the legs hit the rug. I wondered if Carol recognized my fidgetiness in those thumps.

"Maybe they're busy. It *is* September," she said before chuckling. I could tell from the sound that she was right around the corner of our home's hallway. "A lot goes on at the start of a school year," she said.

Then she chuckled again, and I knew why: my quirks. She's been giggling at me—a sweet and softhearted laugh that nudges me out of my geek reveries—for thirty years. Carol chuckled when I refused to slow down at my Shotokan karate "hobby" until I got a black belt (and a bunch of mangled toes). Carol rolled her eyes when I brought along a satellite phone on an Alaskan cruise (to keep in touch with the office). She shook her head after I left Qualcomm a very rich man and decided, in the name of economizing, to work out of the house. Sighing, she'd pointed out that there was no real space in our thirty-year-old, three-bedroom ranch-style house for my home office, and added that she wasn't going to give up her office in our house for me. My wife lets me drive myself crazy-hard. But that doesn't mean she contributes to it. Or tries to keep up.

My home "office" is really just an outpost in our hallway. It's right outside our daughter Rebecca's room and around the corner from Carol's cozy, enclosed workspace, from which she sends e-mails, does charity work, and burns family photos onto discs. I sit at a cramped armoire, with a makeshift desk space barely big enough to fit a laptop, some piles of paper, family snapshots, and a few sticky notes.

I continued thumping the chair legs down on the carpet.

"Why don't you get out with the dog for a walk?" Carol suggested from her office.

The next day the phone rang.

"Hi, Steve. This is Doug Purcell, the principal at Mount Pleasant High School."

I cleared my throat. A response!

"I received a message that you're interested in teaching," he continued.

Something was a little off. I couldn't hear Purcell very well. Was it a bad connection?

We started talking. Purcell spoke slowly, and in a noticeable monotone. Every time he said "teaching," it came out with all the enthusiasm one might use to say "sandpapering."

"Do you know much about our school?" he asked drily.

No, I didn't, I said, trying to be okay with Purcell's phone presence. What was going on with him? Wasn't a high school principal supposed to inspire, acting as motivator, leader, and entertainer? Purcell was flat.

While we spoke, I glanced at the framed photograph of Nolan Ryan hanging next to my desk. Now there was someone, I thought to myself, who could run a public high school. Ryan, the legendary, retired pro baseball pitcher, inspired lots of people. In the picture, he's in the middle of a game and set to make a pitch, despite blood dripping down his chin. The photo was taken just after Ryan had been hit in the face with a line drive that had been smacked by Bo Jackson. Ryan had refused to leave the game. Personally, I hate the sight of my own blood, which also makes Carol chuckle. But every time I look at that picture, I think of Ryan's toughness and determination. It fuels me.

Was Purcell anything like Ryan?

"We have some big challenges here. Perhaps you might find some of them interesting," he said flatly.

We spoke for about fifteen minutes. Even if Purcell sounded odd, I wanted to meet him. It wasn't like other principals were calling.

"Can I come by?" I asked.

We set a date for the following week.

. . .

As the crow flies, Mount Pleasant High is only about fifteen miles from my home. But in terms of economics, the gap is vast. Heading east to meet Purcell for the first time, I passed nearby my neighborhood French bakery and the local Ferrari dealership. Several miles and a couple of highways later, I took the Capitol Expressway exit and drove into what felt like another planet. Signs advertised janitorial supply stores and taquerias. Exhaust hung over ten lanes of inner-city traffic. Yellowing, weedy gardens fronted many of the homes, as did driveways marred by large oil spots or broken-down cars. These were the neighborhoods I could see, anyway. Giant walls obscured some of the blocks I passed. Were they keeping out the city's grit and noise? Or hiding profoundly sad lives?

After thirty minutes of driving, I pulled up to the school in my Lexus. On first look the place passed for a neighborhood oasis. Mature shade trees enhance Mount Pleasant's façade, and the main building sits atop a knoll of manicured grass. The facility is set well back from a heavily trafficked intersection.

Up close, however, Mount Pleasant's personality was different. The main, one-story building was painted a surly brown, and gave off all the warmth of a barracks. A big portal onto the campus was shadowy, like the entrance to a cave. There were metal security gates. The obvious way into the structure was through a set of beefy doors.

Purcell's office wasn't far from the building's entrance. His secretary waved me toward his doorway, which Purcell filled before I entered. He definitely didn't look like the Nolan Ryan of high school principals. Purcell was short, pale, and balding. He was fifty-five and stood with a slight stoop. Is that what a lifetime of working in public education does for a man? Wears him out?

"Ah, you made the crossing. Come on in," Purcell said, gesturing slowly with his right hand for me to take a seat before he sat down heavily in his desk chair. "Let's talk about what you're interested in doing, Steve. And I'll tell you what Mount Pleasant has to offer."

"I loved school, and I want kids today loving it, too," I said. "I have all this business experience and recently worked in the White House. I'd like to think that if I got into a classroom and was allowed to teach, I could share my passions. I could give students glimpses of worlds that are pretty eye-opening, and at the same time learn about what happens at a high school in the twenty-first century.

"Maybe I could make a difference in some lives," I added, realizing the cliché immediately after I'd said it. "At least a small difference."

Purcell took a moment to absorb my highly enthusiastic pitch. "Yup, you could definitely give the kids a different perspective," he said, nodding while the words came unstuck from his tongue. "Probably some very valuable insights, and it'd be good for the students to know more about the possibilities that are out there. Remind me: How long did you say that you worked in the Valley?"

I described some of the moments I'd had running Strategic Mapping and SnapTrack. I explained that I didn't back away from the challenges I'd encountered, either in California or in Washington, D.C. I'd relished them.

"It's not like I didn't expect difficulties," I said. "I was always careful to consider the hurdles that I thought I'd face. You know, a lot of planning and anticipating. But usually once I make up my mind to face challenges, I plow right in."

Purcell's hands were weakly clasped atop his desk.

"Do you think you could bring that kind of energy here?" he said, with a hint of hope. "I know where folks like you come from. Teaching here wouldn't be like teaching honors classes at some wealthy suburban school. There isn't much discussion at Mount Pleasant about which Ivy League colleges kids will be attending.

We're generally occupied with everyone getting their high school diplomas."

While Purcell spoke, I glanced out the large picture-frame windows that lined one side of his modest office. Students were milling about on the other side of the glass, and I was all at once excited and intimidated by what I saw. Many of the kids outside Purcell's windows were Hispanic or Asian, and I was charged up at the idea of regularly mixing with students who came from diverse social and socioeconomic backgrounds. Such diversity defined California's public schools. In fact, it defined the state. Meanwhile, the Valley that I knew so intimately—while blessed with an international population—hewed to a largely uniform business culture.

"In other words, Steve," Purcell continued, "teaching here could be satisfying for you. It will definitely be different, and hard."

Purcell's delivery remained dull. Yet I noticed something else. His word choices were razor-sharp. Like a sly fox, Purcell was both complimenting and challenging me. He was buttering me up. Purcell even looked the part: He had a fox's long nose and a toothy, mischievous grin.

"The kids can be really disruptive. It'd be tough going, even for someone like you," he said.

"Uncharted territory," he added.

"Your biggest challenge ever," he said, and then sat back. "What do you think? Are you interested?"

Purcell definitely made teaching at Mount Pleasant sound like one of those multiheaded problems that I like to face. I wanted in.

"What would be the next steps?" I said.

Purcell temporarily evaded my queries. We spoke for an hour. He told me about Mount Pleasant's financial challenges—often there wasn't enough money to address basic needs, like fixing a leaky roof or a broken water fountain. Despite his position, he added, he was also limited in the influence he had over his teachers. Those kinds of changes, and many others, came only from upstream in the California educational system, in Sacramento. If they came at all.

"There's a lot I can't control. Go into the classrooms. See for yourself," he said, and suggested that I start by observing. We agreed that I'd attend all sorts of classes—English, math, economics, and others—in order to get a general sense of the material and environment. If, after a few weeks of observing, I remained enthusiastic, Purcell said he would consider finding me a guest-teaching slot.

"And if that goes well?" I asked eagerly, already envisioning my own class. "Then what?"

Purcell wouldn't commit to anything more.

During those sixty minutes of conversation, there were lots of issues begging for further discussion. Issue number one: Why would Purcell give me a chance?

That East Side Union High School District bureaucrat and ten other principals had shrugged me off (no one except Purcell responded to my voice mail messages). Purcell, right from the beginning of our conversation, knew that I had no formal teaching experience. I wasn't convinced that I'd won him over just because of my entrepreneur's enthusiasm for jumping at a challenge, either. Could I really bring something special to his school? There had to be Silicon Valley high school teachers capable of teaching my kind of subject matter. If Purcell had wanted more of a businessperson's perspective, he could've gotten it before I'd offered my services. He'd been Mount Pleasant's principal for five years.

My newfound wealth added to my skepticism. The news of Snap-

Track's billion-dollar sale had made national business headlines. The success story preceded me wherever I went, even if I was meeting someone from a charity or an institution only for an informational interview. It's not that I was uncomfortable being labeled "rich." But I had to wonder if a lot of people were more interested in donations than they were in me.

Indeed, when Purcell brought up Mount Pleasant's cash-flow problems and wafer-thin budgets, and when he warned me of the challenges I'd encounter as a teacher, I wondered if he wasn't just hoping for a contribution. I'm sure he wouldn't have complained if our conversation had left me fearful, and sympathetic to his cash-strapped position. He would have still gained plenty if I'd written him a check and never returned. The subjects of philanthropy and my money, however, never came up.

There was also something intriguing yet unclear about how Purcell thought of me. At one point he'd mentioned seeing me "as a potential opportunity to stir up the system." Over the course of our conversation, I learned that Purcell and I had our similarities: He had always approached education with an entrepreneurial mind-set. During his thirty years in the profession, he'd never just sat back and delivered memorizable lessons. Instead he'd branched out, securing contributions for public school education from companies like Adobe, IBM, and Apple, helping to create federally funded magnet programs (fairly unique school offerings that would attract a diverse student population), and overlaying organizational performance standards from the worlds of business and industry onto teaching.

"What I always find intriguing," Purcell said in our meeting, "is rethinking the way we educate people."

Purcell's surprising gusto sounded great. But I didn't know how I'd "stir up the system." I saw no need to tell him that my experience as an educator amounted to guest lecturing in a first-grade science class. The teacher who brought me in for those duties was my sister-in-law.

I didn't tell Purcell something else either: My potential adventures at Mount Pleasant represented only the start of what I anticipated to be a long-term commitment to public service. What, exactly, was my ultimate goal? Truthfully, I didn't know. Purcell and I had touched on politics—we discovered that we were both Republicans, which put us in the minority among the Mount Pleasant staff. But back then I wasn't thinking about becoming an elected official so much as an agent of change for education. I was at Mount Pleasant to roll up my sleeves because I thought that teaching was the best way to fully understand the problems facing California's public schools. If I were given my own semester-long class to teach at Mount Pleasant, there would be plenty of time for me to consider my next steps, and to have more conversations with Purcell.

The principal wanted to take baby steps with me, too. At the end of our meeting, Purcell got up and walked me to the door. "Come back next Monday and we'll start you observing some classes," he said, patting me on the shoulder. "That's when we'll get to know each other."

I was relieved to find my Lexus as I'd left it. Before arriving at Mount Pleasant earlier in the day, East San Jose's landscape had seemed foreign, but riveting. On my way out, however, the shadows grew longer, and the surroundings became scary. Opening the door to my car, I noticed a residential street just over the school parking lot's fence. There was an old Cadillac resting on two flat tires. Something smelled rotten, like trash that had sat around too long. A dog's raspy bark sounded uncomfortably close.

The San Jose area has long endured an east-west polarization. The million-person, two-hundred-thirty-year-old city was originally built on agriculture, and César Chávez, before becoming an iconic labor activist, took up residence in San Jose's east side. Specifically, in the 1950s Chavez lived in a San Jose barrio called Sal Si Puedes, which means "escape if you can."

During World War II, the city's industrial base shifted toward technology. San Jose factories built amphibious vehicles for the war, and subsequently created designs and technologies for other combat vehicles, too. IBM opened offices in the city and developed computers and related technology, which attracted engineers and competition. Technology companies also sprouted in other cities west of San Jose, like Sunnyvale, Cupertino, and Campbell. Their increasingly affluent workforces migrated westward. The town where I live, which is directly west of Mount Pleasant, is overwhelmingly white and non-Hispanic. East San Jose, meanwhile, remains a low-income, largely immigrant community.

The school's neighborhood is rough, even when seen through the eyes of someone who's not wealthy and white. Drive-by shootings happen. Kids learn to avoid bumping into strangers at the local convenience stores. Recently, the San Jose Police Department received nearly fifteen times more calls for suspicious vehicles around Mount Pleasant High than in a more affluent San Jose neighborhood. More specifically, in a year's time, police stopped one thousand vehicles in the area. Over that same time frame, the neighborhood generated nearly 850 calls to SJPD dispatchers for disturbances, and 15 for violations by registered sex offenders.

Mount Pleasant serves a largely underprivileged population. The thirty-year-old school's student body is 10 percent Caucasian, the rest being mostly Hispanic and Asian kids. About 20 percent of the students aren't proficient in English, and only one-third of the parents of

Mount Pleasant students either attended some college classes or graduated from a four-year college.

It's no crime for such adults to have decided against higher education—there's nothing wrong with entering the workforce at a younger age and wanting to hold down a solid job and bring up a family. But less-educated parents encounter many hurdles if they want their children to get a college degree. What if those adults are hardworking first-generation Americans who seek a better life for their kids but don't speak enough English to help a daughter or son run the college-entrance gauntlet? What if the students' families or neighbors don't know how to help? Or if the kids don't feel welcome enough on their high school campus to stick around after class and seek out guidance?

Indeed, Mount Pleasant itself could seem like a forbidding place. Students sometimes call the school "Mount Pregnant" (there's school-sponsored child care for student moms), and the kids have to endure anxieties beyond unexpected parenthood (or bad grades or social ostracism). There have been shootings on campus, and at least one murder. There are racial tensions and gangs. In a 2007 poll of East Side Union High School District students, when asked if they felt very safe at school, only 12 percent of the polled eleventh-graders said yes.

Carol didn't need any data to have concerns about my well-being at a tough public high school. She had grown up in San Jose, the oldest daughter of five children in a tight-knit Catholic family. Her mom stayed home to take care of the kids and her dad managed a local bank. Carol's folks didn't have a ton of money. Nonetheless, she grew up in a safe neighborhood and loved school.

"Why don't you give some more thought to this whole idea?" Carol said while pulling a lasagna out of the oven soon after I returned from my meeting with Purcell. "You know, I'm all for you learning about public education. I'm happy for you to go teach at Mount Pleasant, so long as I know you'll be safe. But will you?" she said, setting down the hot cooking dish and pulling off her oven mitts. "Maybe you could start by working your way onto the board of a public school system," she added. "Or by volunteering at Rebecca's school."

Rebecca's school, I reminded Carol, wouldn't shed much light on the state of California's public education system. Rebecca had been in the same private elementary school for years—a great school that she'd first attended when we lived in a part of Silicon Valley where the public schools, I hate to say, were subpar. When we moved into the hills, we decided against transferring her.

"Why don't you call more principals? Aren't there other districts?" Carol persisted. There was no laughing tonight. Instead she kept firing off questions, which is what she does when she's worried. She squared her five-foot-tall body to me, and her brown eyes laser-locked on mine. "It really needs to be *this* school?" she asked.

"Mount Pleasant is the real deal, Carol. A struggling California public high school," I said. "I can't tell you how much I think I'd learn from the classes and this principal, Doug Purcell. At first he seemed oddly uninspired to me. But I actually think he's highly motivated to improve education."

"Maybe you shouldn't drive a showy car there," Carol said, twisting her wedding band around her finger. She was searching for a smaller victory in what she knew was a losing battle. Long ago, my wife decided that when she can't beat me, she'll join me. Which is why she volunteered to be company secretary in the early days of Strategic Mapping. Maybe, Carol thought back then, her contribution would mean that my business partners wouldn't spend so many nights on our couches.

"Why don't you go buy a clunker?" she added.

"Carol, I don't drive a Rolls. The Lexus is a sedan. It's not new."

"Why call attention to yourself?" she said. "What if someone wants you, and not the car?"

Carol knows the value of life better than I do. She was born with a heart defect and almost died as a child. She has had numerous surgeries. As an adult, she has battled and beaten breast cancer. She's grateful for every single day on earth. Meanwhile, the worst thing I've ever endured is tumbling off a moped as a teenager. I've never broken a bone. Relative to my wife, I take life for granted.

Unfortunately, Carol's concerns about something as crazy as abduction occasionally haunted me, too. Back in early 2000, the *San Jose Mercury News* had virtually screamed that I'd struck it rich by selling SnapTrack: SAN JOSE START-UP SOLD FOR $1 BILLION, read the headline. You see your name all over a story like that and your mind occasionally goes to strange places. What if some band of crazies went after me, or my family? I hated having such paranoid thoughts. I tried hard to ignore them. Really hard.

"If I start teaching at Mount Pleasant, I'll be mindful," I assured Carol between bites of lasagna. "I'll be careful."

The next Monday was my first day of high school in thirty years. I packed a bag lunch and showed up bright and early at Mount Pleasant, ready to go.

"Good morning," said Purcell, getting up from behind his desk. "Follow me." And we walked through Mount Pleasant's unremarkable administrative building. There was dust on the glass sports trophy case. Framed honor roll lists hung askew on the wall.

As we walked into an atrium, the nostalgia washed over me: High school remained a lot like I remembered it. Classrooms and lockers framed lots of open spaces that were lit up with bronze autumn sun and patches of mowed green grass. School was between periods, and Purcell and I weaved past students wearing high-tops, jeans, and backpacks. They were laughing and joking. Some hidden voice delivered a garbled message about cross-country running over the school's public-address system.

Purcell guided me into a classroom. There were about thirty desks facing the front of the room, and a Shakespeare quote was written in large lettering above the words *tragedy, comedy, novel,* and *play* on a whiteboard.

Purcell and I slid behind desks at the back of the room. After all the students filed in and the door was closed, the room became quite dark. Thick brown paper was sloppily taped across a good portion of the floor-to-ceiling windows. I leaned over to Purcell and asked him why it was there.

"The big windows are distracting. They invite students to look out or look in," he explained, sotto voce. "Some of the teachers cover 'em up. Helps the kids focus."

Bathed in the harsh light of overhead fluorescent bulbs, the space was as uninviting as an interrogation room. I looked around and noticed that a lot of the desks were mismatched, and the carpeting was worn. When the teacher—a sturdy-looking, middle-aged man—cleared his throat to get the kids' attention, I held my breath. What kind of educational horror film was about to play? Would I see spitballs? Students dancing on their desks? Anarchy?

But the unexpected happened. The class quickly quieted down, and the teacher cheerfully launched into a lecture on how to approach reading literature. There was a lively debate about the benefits of reading fast (one gets through the assigned work quickly) versus slowly (it takes more time, but the reading takes on more rhythm and meaning). Plenty of students raised their hands to comment. Enthusiasm remained high even after the teacher transitioned to a talk on grammar. The class seemed pretty great to me, and I said as much to Purcell.

"Glad you enjoyed it," he said, getting up from the desk. "We're just warming up."

For the next couple of weeks, Purcell had me observe additional classes in English, and some in math, too. To my uneducated eye, they were all respectable.

Then one day Purcell escorted me to a fifth-period economics class, taught by a teacher named Robert Wald. "This will be different than what you've been seeing. Up to now they've all been honors-type classes," Purcell told me as we walked toward the social sciences classrooms.

Okay, I thought. Now what?

"This is a required class for seniors," he said, some drama conveniently built into his sluggish delivery. "*Regular* seniors."

Wald happened to be standing outside his classroom when we approached. He seemed to be about thirty years old, and had the broad shoulders and thick neck of someone you'd want on your side in a schoolyard brawl. He didn't smile or frown.

"Robert, this is Steve Poizner," said Purcell. "Steve, this is Robert Wald."

He had a strong handshake. "I'm happy for you to sit in on the class," Wald said. His voice was deep. "Please don't interrupt."

Unfortunately, plenty of other people in Wald's class did interrupt. Wald wasn't five minutes into an explanation of supply and demand before a boy with the trace of a mustache quipped, "Here's what I know: I better be supplied when I demand something."

Kids laughed. "Sshhhh," said Wald, before seamlessly returning to his lecture.

Then a girl used her tongue to snap the gum she was chewing.

"Marissa!" Wald interjected, and her mouth ceased moving.

"I can't concentrate," announced another girl, and Wald pretended not to hear her. To his credit, he kept rolling, never becoming undone.

After class ended, I watched the kids spill out into the atrium. Delivering that lecture would have completely frustrated me.

"Nice work," I said to Wald after class. "Kind of a tough crowd."

"You get used to it," said Wald with a shrug, and he then explained that he had somewhere to be. We went our separate ways.

I spent the next two weeks attending Wald's class, and other social sciences classes, too. They were sobering—the kids were frequently lackluster about their work. But I thought that if I did get an opportunity to teach, the social sciences department would be my home. It was responsible for instructing Mount Pleasant's students in both business and civics. Too bad that aside from Wald's occasional post-class color commentary and some abbreviated conversations with his peers, I didn't feel terribly welcome.

I tried to figure out the department's collective cold shoulder. Many of the teachers taught five classes per day, which came to about 150 kids. Maybe they didn't have the energy to make nice with me. Or did they think I would bail out at a difficult moment? Or maybe they figured that I was full of myself, as if there were anyone who could, with the snap of a finger, reverse the fortunes of whatever he addressed—be it a technology, a business, or a school.

Turns out that to a certain extent, all of my notions were accurate. One day in October, maybe a month after I'd begun my daily ritual of observing classes, Purcell called me into his office.

"We've had entrepreneurs before you commit to teaching," he said, his arms crossed. "We've been disappointed. One of them really burned Wald. He kept backing out of his commitments."

I was preparing to champion myself when Purcell went on.

"However, you've shown up every day, Steve. You seem genuinely interested. You're also willing to listen," he said. "I could come to regret this offer." "but we're impressed enough to let you guest-teach classes for a couple of weeks. Robert says you can work with his economics class. Think you can explain how to start a company?"

Now I had to teach. Observing Mount Pleasant's classes for a month had demonstrated to me that teaching wasn't anything like running a company of Silicon Valley engineers. On-the-job professionals, even difficult ones, pay some attention to their bosses. At Mount Pleasant, at least outside of the honors classes I had attended, students often behaved as if listening to the teacher was optional. What would I do if the class got unruly? I have a soft spot for innocents, like kids and dogs. Even when we're arguing, Rebecca can squeeze me for an ice cream cone. As for Jake, my old golden retriever: I couldn't consistently bring myself to keep him off our living room couch.

I asked Purcell how he thought I should approach the class. I'd seen some Mount Pleasant teachers lecture through the whole period, and others make their classes interactive. Also, not long after leaving Qualcomm, I'd visited classes at some other public schools, and seen teachers who taught with near-hyperbolic amounts of energy. What kind of teacher should I be?

Purcell shrugged. He had big-picture advice.

"Focus on learning, not just teaching content," he said. "All too often I see teaching boil down to memorization and regurgitation. You want to create critical thinkers. Challenge them to think," he said.

Challenge them, I repeated to myself. Create critical thinkers.

On a Monday in late October, I stood behind the teacher's desk and watched about thirty kids file into Wald's classroom. A couple of other social sciences teachers grabbed seats, too. Wald introduced me as a Silicon Valley businessman who was interested in leading some classes. Then the floor was mine. I was nervous.

I spoke briefly about myself—my education, my experiences as an entrepreneur, and how I'd worked in the White House and spent time with President George W. Bush. I showed a slide of me shaking the president's hand. I also explained that I would be teaching Mr. Wald's class for a short stretch. My subject was starting a business.

I took a deep breath.

"What is an entrepreneur?" I asked, standing in front of the class. "A person who takes chances to create a new product or develop a better way to deliver a service," I said.

"Someone who's willing to risk failure," I added, and heard the spoken words in my head. They sounded wooden.

"Someone who's not satisfied until the mission is accomplished," I said, doing a quick visual sweep of the room. Apparently I wasn't accomplishing much. Two kids were looking at each other from across the room and smirking. A girl was twirling her hair with her pinkie, and staring into space.

"Someone who's willing to make an almost supernatural commitment to what seems impossible by most others," I continued.

I lectured a while longer and then decided to get some feedback. To *challenge* the kids.

"Any questions so far?" I asked.

Nobody raised a hand. Some students giggled. Was I that bad? Was my fly unzipped?

I soldiered on, feeling like I was stiffening right before the students' and teachers' eyes. I explained that people start new businesses for all sorts of reasons, and went through the multiple steps to become a successful entrepreneur.

I was thankful when the fifty-minute period came to an end. I quickly gave out my e-mail address and invited the students to write to me. Like they'd have anything to ask, I thought.

As soon as I got home I plopped onto the couch. Jake was next to me. He licked my chin. Carol leaned against the kitchen counter, her arms crossed.

"Taught like a true rookie," I said. "I'm not sure one word of the lecture sunk in." I wondered aloud how long I'd take to loosen up in the classroom, and if becoming an entrepreneur was in any of Mount Pleasant students' thoughts. Were they all too busy ducking bullets to consider their careers? I felt out of step—a privileged brainiac who didn't know how to teach, and had little understanding of his students' sensibilities. Talk about a wall.

"Just your first day," Carol said. "You'll figure it out."

She was right. I'd had many dark moments at Strategic Mapping and SnapTrack, and I knew better than to get bogged down by them. There was always a chance to redeem oneself. Still, going from Valley chieftain to East Side newbie wasn't fun.

I checked my e-mail before going to bed that night, and up popped a letter from one of the kids in class.

> Hello Mr. Poizner,
> I want to know more about what you do and I was
> wandering if you can teach me how to meet with the
> president too. I will see you in class than.

I didn't know whether to be happy that this boy had written or disappointed by the fact that he saw me as an "in" at the White House.

Plus, for a kid who must've been seventeen or eighteen years old, he wrote and spelled terribly. What could a teacher at Mount Pleasant really hope to accomplish?

I slid my fingers behind my glasses, and rubbed my eyes. Then I closed the letter and powered down for the night.

Purcell called me into his office before I taught class for a third day. He assured me that everything was fine. I hadn't crumbled. The kids hadn't revolted.

"Have some fun. Make the curriculum come alive," he said in a monotone that clashed with his upbeat advice. "Get creative."

I thought I had a decent idea in the works. The day before, I'd tried to home in on what I loved most about being an entrepreneur. What had made me leave Boston Consulting Group, and always kept me going at Strategic Mapping and SnapTrack? Of course my companies were businesses, and they invented significant technologies and provided people with jobs. Those were all real motivators. But why else had I launched my companies?

They were challenges. And what were challenges if not stimulating. Fun. *Games.* The start-up industry has very clear-cut rules and winners and losers. In the simplest terms, my long working hours in Silicon Valley had been filled with games—even if they were played with adult metrics, sophisticated concepts, and clenched jaws.

Soon I walked into Wald's classroom with a couple of shopping bags and a lesson designed for the students to apply themselves instead of just unconsciously scribbling notes while I lectured. They would become entrepreneurs.

"You're all about to compete in a game," I said. "You're starting your own companies. You'll have to market products and sell them, too."

I divided the class into a half dozen smaller groups, and reached into the bags. Out came the cheap, similarly priced electronics I'd picked up at Best Buy—headphones, a low-end CD player, a couple of different portable radios. Each group, I explained, had to sell an item on eBay. The team that sold its product for the highest price won.

"You'll have to make some key decisions," I explained. "How will you display the item? What's the right asking price?"

There were murmurs in the classroom. At first I wanted to quiet everyone. But the kids weren't distracted. They were into the idea.

"Dude, we should say the headphones will blow out people's eardrums!" said one boy with a giant hoop earring in his right ear.

"That's not gonna attract buyers," argued his friend. "That's stupid."

The students debated over which digital photos were best for displaying their items online. Should they picture the headphones being worn by someone or on a plain background? Should the CD player be shown with compact discs? If so, what kind of music would appeal to the most affluent audience? Classical? Opera? Nine Inch Nails? Without the aid of a textbook or PowerPoint presentation, my students were getting a genuine lesson in marketing and promotion. They were considering demographics and pricing strategies.

After posting the items on eBay, we logged on to the Internet daily to see what items had received bids, and for how much. Several days later, I announced the winning team, which had sold the CD player for about thirty-seven dollars. The classroom was pretty charged—there were high fives and shaking heads. Meanwhile, some kids were still staring off into space.

But I felt empowered. The eBay game was my first indication that I could reach these kids. They learned from me! One evening during the contest, a student sent me a satisfying e-mail:

It is an honor Mr. Poizner to be having you as a guest

teacher. You are very well organized and a good speaker.

I hope your dreams come true about becoming a teacher.

Toward the end of my brief gig, I was sitting at Wald's desk after class, which made me feel that much more like a bona fide teacher. I'd been reflecting on how the profession could be so satisfying. Until Wald walked into the room.

His cheeks were flushed, and his brown eyes unblinking and stunned. I'd never seen him off-kilter.

"What's going on?" I asked.

"I broke up a fight," he said, groaning.

"What? Where?" I asked.

"On campus, not far from here. There were two boys. One of them was totally obnoxious," said Wald, sitting at a student desk and taking a few deep breaths to collect himself. "I pulled him away from the other kid. Who knows what they would've done to each other."

Twelve years earlier, in 1990, a sixteen-year-old student from another high school walked onto the Mount Pleasant campus carrying a grudge as well as a gun. He fired into a crowd during a morning recess, killing a freshman. One of the boys involved was Vietnamese, and the other white. The shooting was attributed to racial tension. The event is etched into the institutional memory of the school.

"I have to go talk to Purcell," said Wald.

But before he left, the classroom phone rang. Wald answered and someone on the other end began yelling at him—I could tell by the way Wald held the phone away from his ear. Wald never raised his voice, but he looked stunned all over again.

"That was a dad of one of the kids. Of one of the boys that I just peeled from that fight," he said, setting down the phone. "He's threatening to sue me. He said he'd beat me up and get me fired."

"You did the right thing, Robert," I said. "That dad is a jerk."

"I have to go talk to Purcell," Wald repeated, and then he left the room.

I gathered my things off Wald's desk. Twenty minutes ago I couldn't wait for tomorrow to come so that I could teach again. Now I was thinking that maybe Carol was right. Where could I get a good deal on a clunker?

What was it like to be a teacher, or a young woman, or a small freshman, or even a gangbanger senior, on this campus? Did all such folks, not just at Mount Pleasant but also at struggling public schools across the nation, look over their shoulders every day of the school year? Was there a story behind the fight that Wald had just ended? Did it justify the actions of the battling kids? Of the angry father? Could anyone at Mount Pleasant stop long enough to reflect on the sad state of affairs when fear coexists so closely with learning?

For a second, I wondered if I should just stay in bed tomorrow.

But who was I kidding? I had entered my own game—scaling Mount Pleasant. I knew I'd be back in the morning.

CHAPTER 3

Square Peg

Mount Pleasant's room 600 is surrounded by a dozen or so social sciences classrooms and hordes of students. It's officially known as the "social sciences office," and it's sometimes called a lounge, but it's really more of a refuge. The space is nearly windowless. For a few precious minutes at lunchtime each day, teachers retreat to room 600. They come to be with their own, to catch their collective breath. They don't want to deal with kids. Or strangers, like me.

"Hey, Ian. How come you didn't buy me one of those?" Wald asked Ian Ellison, a tall man with a gentle-giant disposition who, like Wald, taught economics and civics. Ellison took another bite of his deli sandwich, which was wrapped in paper from Togo's, and offered no response. He was thoroughly enjoying his meal while reading a sports magazine. "You know, I'm hungry, too," Wald added.

It was a rainy day in early November, a few weeks before the

Thanksgiving break, and there were nearly a dozen of us seated around a collection of tables all pushed together. Randall Nuñez, who had been teaching in the social sciences department for around thirty years, flipped through a newspaper covered with gloomy headlines about the threat of war in Iraq. Sally Constell, the social sciences department head, sipped from a bowl of soup hot out of the microwave. Barbara Stevens, a health and wellness teacher, ate a spinach salad. Dustin Martz, a kid of twenty-five and a recent addition to the math program, crunched on some pretzels while grading tests. Like a handful of other teachers from various departments at Mount Pleasant, Martz was welcome at the room 600 lunch circle.

And then there was me. I'd started coming to lunches in the lounge a month or so earlier. Wald had invited me, probably as a courtesy after I kept peppering him with questions about teaching and working in the California public school system. I took him up on his offer immediately, even though the teachers remained wary of me. Just because Purcell found me to be a novelty didn't mean his staff felt the same way.

One day I overheard a snippet of a particularly sobering conversation between Wald and another teacher. "Purcell must have dollar signs in his eyes," Wald had said. "He told me not to screw up with Steve."

I'd been on the periphery before—really, I've been an outsider working to fit in my whole life. But I've made friends almost everywhere I've gone, and I was optimistic that I could find common ground with Mount Pleasant's teachers, too. In due time, anyway.

"Anyone skiing over the holiday?" I asked the teachers seated around the tables. Nuñez kept reading his paper. Constell shrugged. Judy Falcon, a music instructor, explained that she and her family were staying home.

"We're watching our pennies," she said between bites of an apple. "We'll celebrate at our place."

What a dumb question, I thought to myself. The area's public school teacher wages start at around forty thousand dollars. How many of these folks pause to consider ski-chalet vacations?

"Are you going to the mountains?" Falcon politely responded to me, getting up from a table to gently kick a garbage can two inches in one direction. "All this moisture has to mean snow at Lake Tahoe."

I decided to change the subject.

"Is that a new leak?" I asked, and a few teachers joined me in looking up at the water-stained ceiling. Room 600 leaked a lot. One of the roof's holes was now dripping water from a new spot. Falcon centered the trash can precisely under the drops, and then surveyed the additional garbage cans in the room that doubled as rain barrels. Several of us looked at one another and shook our heads.

When the conversation turned to tough conditions—weather, budgetary, working—my input was heard and often welcomed.

I'd needed only a few minutes into my first visit to recognize the sorry state of the lounge. There were the water stains and burned-out lightbulbs. The copy machine was broken. The furniture was mismatched, old, and worn. It looked like stuff from Goodwill's reject pile.

"What happened to the maxim that education is one of a community's highest priorities?" I'd asked aloud. We'd enter sarcastic conversations about how Mount Pleasant wasn't in Calcutta but rather the Silicon Valley, with all of its wealth, prosperity, and venture capital.

"Tell the people you know that we jump through hoops to get the copy machine repaired. And the roof always needs fixing," Constell said to me soon after I started attending lounge lunches. "Tell them the department works on an annual budget of about a thousand dollars."

I know the value of a buck. Carol rolls her eyes because I like to fly coach. Still, no functioning copy machine for an entire department? Social sciences teachers had to go to great lengths just to copy tests or worksheets. I also noticed that the classrooms didn't have projectors that could show PowerPoint presentations. What century were we in? Or was I hopelessly out of touch?

"We just want to do our jobs," Wald once told me. "When it comes to improving conditions at Mount Pleasant, we're agnostic. We don't care who helps us—volunteer, administrator, politician. Just so long as something gets done."

Politicians and politics came up more and more often at lunch. As a group, the social sciences department leaned way left. But the teachers generally respected me because I listened to their arguments and tried my best to give thoughtful answers.

Most of the teachers respected me, anyway. Simon Delaney was another story.

Delaney was an English teacher and had been at Mount Pleasant for half a dozen years. He was also a hard-core Democrat. He'd been an enthusiastic volunteer for the Democratic party and displayed the same kind of deep passion for Democrats as a football-crazed, cheese-head hat–wearing Wisconsinite shows for the Green Bay Packers.

Delaney seemed to quote reporting from C-SPAN verbatim, and on any given day he could tell me missteps he thought the Republican party had made within the last twenty-four-hour news cycle. He gave me the impression that my party was synonymous with political maneuvering performed solely to benefit the rich. If principal Purcell was a shrewd old fox, then Delaney, who was dark, short, and slightly round, with rings under his eyes, approximated a raccoon: benign looks covering unpredictable—really mercurial—behavior. Sometimes I felt like my just being in his presence would set him off. He'd ask me ridiculous, open-ended questions, and I came to think that Delaney believed that I'd been planted at Mount Pleasant. Like I was a spy working in cahoots with President Bush and Karl Rove.

"How did you get here?" Delaney had said to me at one of my first lunches in room 600, backing away as if I had pneumonia. "Didn't you come to us straight from the White House?"

He also happily informed me that he regularly lunched in the social sciences lounge. He and the teachers in the department, he said, had *lots* of shared values. From time to time, Delaney succeeded in making me feel like the consummate outsider. I often wondered if I would remember my stretch at Mount Pleasant as a time when I was never quite accepted.

Delaney's intelligence only made the situation more frustrating. He was quite smart and a good teacher. I'd observed a few of his classes, and they were solid. He also respected that I'd served as a White House Fellow. We entered into enough good conversations that I occasionally thought we were turning a corner.

But like I said, the guy was a raccoon in teacher's clothing. I'd go home and grumble to Carol: Which Delaney would show up for lunch the next day? The intellectual willing to have an interesting chat, or the liberal wanting to claw me to ribbons?

"I like you, but I can't believe in your politics," he'd say, and dismissively wave me off. He refused to separate person from party.

I could only imagine that the other lunchtime regulars sometimes wondered which Delaney would sit down at the table, too. While his peers seemed to sometimes tire of him, they also apparently appreciated Delaney's outspokenness. He asked the questions nobody else dared to. Plus, his unpredictability turned room 600 gatherings into Shakespearean theater.

On that rainy November day, I wasn't halfway through the bag of Fritos that Carol had packed for me when Delaney came through the lounge door.

"Had to talk to a student," he said, pulling up a chair and opening his brown bag. Sally Constell got up and nudged another of the drip-catching garbage cans with her sneaker. Ellison and Wald slowly unfolded the Ping-Pong table that they often used for a game or three that would last through a good part of almost every lunch break.

Delaney looked up from his lunch and saw me.

"Oh, Steve, hi," he said. He took a bite of his sandwich.

"I just want to know how you live with yourself, working for *that* party," Delaney added, licking his lips. "You know, are you sure that *your* president in the White House has the answers to terrorism? Are we really safe? What do you have to say?"

Does anyone have the right replies to such questions? I sure didn't. Nonetheless, all eyes in the room turned to me.

In my early days of teaching, progress in the classroom felt linear, although at Mount Pleasant everything was relative. The students were responding to me at a pace approximating two steps forward and one step back.

"How does inflation affect our lives?" I asked one November day while guest-teaching another one of Wald's economics classes. A short boy who seemed to be paying little attention raised his hand.

I pointed to him.

"I talked about inflation last night with my dad," he said. "He told me that when he was a kid, candy bars were a dime. Now they're, like, ten times as much money. So now we need more money."

"You mean money isn't worth as much?" I asked.

"Yeah, that's what I mean," he replied. "Too bad. I'd be a lot richer with what I have."

The kid was on the right track. I felt like I was, too.

Wald and Purcell had both deemed my eBay lesson plan a success. They rewarded me with more responsibility. Suddenly I was teaching three of Wald's five economics classes per day. It was only for a couple of weeks, but the pressure was on. I was at Mount Pleasant for a good chunk of the day, and I'd come home and have to grade papers and tests. Then I'd have to organize the next day's lesson plan for as many as one hundred students.

"Do you want to watch *The West Wing* while we eat?" Carol said while passing me at my hallway desk one night. I'd come home with a lot of schoolwork.

She had made tacos for dinner. Mexican food is my favorite, and to my remarkably unsophisticated palate, Carol's cooking runs a close second only to Taco Bell's.

I also felt the pull of the television and the den. When the three Poizners want to be lazy, we eat in front of the TV. Rebecca and I love slapstick comedy—the dumber, the better. Carol likes romance and drama. We all enjoyed *The West Wing*.

"Come on, Dad. You can work later," said Rebecca, skipping up to the desk. Her lively brown eyes and playful grin always seem to be scheming for ways to distract me. Indeed, Rebecca is the one person who can consistently lure me away from my work, to play cards, watch Will Ferrell movies (over and over), or go to Dave & Buster's, our favorite gaming arcade. Even when I labored away at SnapTrack, I'd spend every Saturday doing something fun with Rebecca.

"I finished my homework," Rebecca said with an optimistic lift in her voice, convinced she was about to hook me. She bounced her fidgety body against my desk chair, and gathered her long, rope-thick brown hair into a ponytail.

"*I* have homework to do," I said. "We'd better eat in the kitchen."

The decision didn't resonate with Carol and Rebecca. When it comes to watering the plants or cleaning up after the dog, the two of them are happy to empower me. But as for me being king of my castle?

They ate in the den. I ate at my desk.

I graded papers. I had asked the students to write out what types of companies might tempt them to invest their money, and one kid wrote, "A medical company. Because people will always be sick."

"Great start," I wrote on the homework, resisting the impulse to say that I had hoped for a much more detailed answer. "Can you think of more specifics? What kind of medical-related company might be in great demand? What illnesses need a lot of care and attention?"

Honestly, the kids and I were sometimes worlds apart. Earlier in the week, for example, I had made a bad assumption. During a lecture I'd used the term *VC* a few times, and as the period came to a close I realized that I'd lost my audience. One girl was checking out her mascara in a compact mirror. A boy was telling another that VC stood for "Viet Cong," and the two then launched into a full-volume debate over the best Vietnam movies of all time. Kids were calling out *"Apocalypse Now"* and *"Full Metal Jacket"* before I regained control of the class.

When I asked if anyone knew that VC also stood for "venture capital," I got blank stares. Nobody had a clue. Plus the students couldn't imagine entrusting some random person who had an idea and little else with millions of investment dollars.

The next day I had to backtrack in all of my economics classes, to explain a term that privileged children in the Valley had been hearing since they were in the womb.

Could it be, I thought to myself while sitting at the desk, that I'd never relate very well to the Mount Pleasant kids? I pushed my dinner plate away from my laptop, realizing that Carol and Rebecca had already squeezed in two hours of TV. I still had to nail down the next day's lesson. How was I going to connect with the students tomorrow?

I wanted to start what I hoped would be a lively conversation about becoming an entrepreneur. History, after all, has proven that entrepreneurial success can come from humble beginnings: The Valley's own Steve Jobs and Steve Wozniak, for instance, began Apple in a garage.

But what if the students hadn't heard of Jobs? Did most of Mount Pleasant's kids have computers at home? If the name Jobs was foreign, then all the air would be taken out of the lesson. I kept thinking. Bill Gates? Larry Ellison? Jerry Yang? They could be complete mysteries, too.

I looked at the clock. Almost eleven.

My eyes drifted over to a half-eaten taco still sitting on my plate. What about, I thought, the birthing story behind . . . Taco Bell?

But I didn't know that story.

I did know the history of Kentucky Fried Chicken. "Colonel" Harland Sanders was broke and at retirement age when he began franchising his restaurants. It was a rags-to-riches anecdote that had nothing to do with my Silicon Valley expertise. The Colonel, however, was a fast-food icon. All the students would know the brand and learn an unlikely tale.

The next day's class went great.

Not a week later, Purcell joined the chorus. At Mount Pleasant, he told me, I needed to become less of a square peg.

"You're obviously trying. And you're improving. You've definitely shown me that you really want to teach a class next spring," said

Purcell. His left index finger tapped steadily on his tidy desk, as if the principal needed a reminder that he worked to his own beat. "But you're not a trained teacher, Steve. You need to get a credential. Otherwise I can't put you in a classroom."

Despite Delaney's polarizing comments and my struggles to connect with Mount Pleasant's kids, I wasn't about to quit my pursuit of a real public-school teaching experience. I had nearly won over Purcell—and was grateful and satisfied to hear his compliment. I'd never been closer to getting my own class.

Sure enough, the California Commission on Teacher Credentialing requires that prospective teaching candidates have a "Single Subject Teaching Credential" to teach full-time without regular in-class supervision. And the more time I spent at Mount Pleasant, the more I appreciated the fact that not just anyone can walk into a classroom and stand at the blackboard—including me. I was quickly learning that successfully motivating students, conveying information, and managing a class are constant challenges. In retrospect, I felt that the school district bureaucrat who had rejected me back in September wasn't wrong for thinking that I was a little nuts.

But while I have plenty of respect for anyone holding a credential or even a master's degree (let alone a PhD) in education, I wondered if such additional studies or even specific credentialing should be the only permissible path for those who want to teach. What about closely mentoring someone who's obviously motivated, and already educated, but not credentialed? Might that approach, on a case-by-case basis, work? Personally, I felt like I had already learned a lot—from Purcell and Wald in particular. And in my own mind, the idea of earning any more academic stripes so that I could teach clashed with my impatient sensibilities. I wanted to work my way into Mount Pleasant ASAP.

Luckily there's a seam in the state teaching commission's policy. I could apply for an "Emergency 30-Day Substitute Teaching Permit," which initially sounded pretty comical to me. I imagined such a permit holder wearing surgeon scrubs and a mask and bursting into a classroom just before the bell rang. As for the thirty-day limitation, Purcell said he could get me the necessary extensions.

There is actually nothing funny about the emergency teaching permit. It exists in part because California teacher turnover rates are staggering. About 20 percent of the state's new teachers quit their jobs within three years of entering the classroom. California's urban areas suffer more, as nearly 50 percent of their new teachers quit within five years. In other words, there are lots of holes in California public schools, and they aren't all in the roofs.

The biggest reason for the exodus? California teachers are overwhelmed. The state's public schools (kindergarten through twelfth grade) are charged with educating more than 6 million kids annually—a number that grew more than 50 percent between 1980 and 2005, when immigrants and U.S. citizens alike poured into the state. The education infrastructure hasn't kept up (California's student numbers are unprecedented; the state has 2 million more schoolkids than Texas public schools, which are the country's second most populous). As a result, California schools rank last in the nation in staff-to-student ratios.

Statistically speaking, the schools don't fare well at attracting new teaching talent, either. Predictably, the harder the job becomes, the fewer people that want to do it, and thus the tougher it gets to find good candidates: Between 2002 and 2007, the number of teaching credentials issued in California fell by almost 30 percent.

But I still wanted in, and the emergency permit was my ticket. (Amazingly, in California's defense, only 5 percent of all teachers are classified as "underprepared"—like those who enter the profession via emergency permits. But that percentage still equals fifteen thousand teachers statewide.) To receive the permit, I had to pay a few bucks and submit my fingerprints and school transcripts to the state. I also had to take a 102-question test called CBEST, or the California Basic Educational Skills Test.

I understood that the CBEST required that I was proficient in basic math, reading, and writing. I wasn't worried until I read on the Internet about a guy who'd been hired by a California school as an assistant principal but couldn't take the job because he failed the test. He proceeded to fail the CBEST nine more times over the next five years. Others who had missed the cut had hired lawyers, who threatened to file a lawsuit against California in the United States Supreme Court. The plaintiffs argued that the test was quirky, racially prejudiced, and illogical, and that it failed to measure candidates' true abilities to head a class.

Carol sighed when I came home with a copy of *Cracking the CBEST.* But I didn't want to take any chances. It could take months for my completed application to be processed. I wanted to pass the test on my first try.

On a cloudy day in November, I took the CBEST in an anonymous county government building in San Jose. I soon realized that I'd let myself fall prey to Web hype—sure, I had to think way back to answer the geometry and grammar questions, and I remain a terrible speller. Even so, I passed.

Purcell assured me that the state education bureaucrats would permit me to teach for an entire semester as long as I worked under a mentor. Wald, who was warming up to me, agreed to take responsibility. I'd teach his twelfth-grade American Government class.

At least on paper, I thought I'd legitimately earned a spot on Mount Pleasant's social sciences crew. Then a faculty member who did some staff counseling called me into her office. I'd never met the woman. Her face had a sad look. What now, I thought? What else does a highly motivated, sufficiently intelligent guy have to do to get some work around here?

"Mr. Poizner, before the new semester starts I suggest that you attend a weeklong workshop on classroom management," she said. Then the woman leaned toward me, as if she were about to unload the deal breaker. "We can only pay you eight dollars an hour to attend," she murmured apologetically.

My whole body relaxed. One of the few instances, I thought, when it wasn't so bad to be out of step.

"You don't need to pay me," I said. "I would be happy to attend."

After Thanksgiving, Purcell told me to create a plan for the spring 2003 semester. Finally, I thought. An educator's task that isn't foreign to me. Now was my chance to show everyone that bringing me on would benefit the students and the school. I'd prove to my peers that I belonged.

During my business career I'd written out many strategic plans, which detailed the development of businesses like Strategic Mapping and SnapTrack. In SnapTrack's case, the strategic plan ultimately shaped a billion-dollar company. I thought I was up to the task of designing a six-month civics course for about thirty kids.

One day in early December, Wald handed me the eight-hundred-page textbook for Mount Pleasant's American Government class, and a copy of a dutiful, eighty-two-point state document titled "History–Social Science Content Standards for California Public Schools."

"Good luck," he said.

That night I sat at my hallway office and flipped through the material.

I could have easily been overwhelmed by the details: federalism and interest groups, the Constitution and Congress, the presidency and civil rights. Where did one start?

I learned long ago: by stepping back and seeking the big picture first. When I launched SnapTrack, I knew that the company couldn't flourish without first developing a central premise, or mission statement. Sounds simple enough, and the phrase "mission statement" has transcended the world of enterprising business. Nowadays Laundromat owners and convenience store managers jot down mission statements.

But developing a mission statement that captures an ambitious vision or higher purpose requires work. In the case of SnapTrack, I knew that we had a breakthrough application of global positioning system technology. I also knew that we had to painstakingly analyze data and options to see how we could best employ our concept.

Should we have put GPS in eighteen-wheelers? Trains? On prison inmates? Dolphins? Being a typical entrepreneur, I wanted our idea to reach the widest possible audience. Only after months of testing, head scratching, and drama did Krasner have the epiphany to place the technology into mobile phones. A messy but unavoidable process ultimately led to SnapTrack's beautifully streamlined mission statement: "To be able to locate a cell phone in an emergency."

The words "global positioning system" didn't even show up.

I then built SnapTrack's strategic plan around our statement. The mission statement informed the patents we sought, partnerships we considered, and employees we interviewed.

Fast-forward to the weeks before I was to inherit my own classroom of high school seniors. Sitting at my desk, I asked myself the same question as a teacher that I'd asked as an entrepreneur: What are your goals?

I'd already been through a messy data-accumulating process—

otherwise known as Mount Pleasant's fall 2002 semester. I'd discovered that the students liked to participate (the eBay game), and were turned off by the esoteric (my lecture on venture capitalists). They loved course material—like KFC's Colonel Sanders—that somehow overlapped with their lives.

I'd received input from other sources, too. Purcell repeatedly told me to push kids to think through and understand concepts. During the limited time I'd spent observing classes outside of Mount Pleasant at a few standout Bay Area public high schools, I'd watched teachers pour massive amounts of energy into their classes. They often got their students to respond similarly. I also couldn't forget about the state's demands. My students had to learn the basics of U.S. government.

After hours spent at the laptop over the course of a few evenings, one night I pushed my chair away from the desk. I had created a three-part mission statement for the class. I was so excited to start teaching that I had goose bumps. I read my work to Carol:

1. Teach students how to formulate informed opinions about problems that are important to them and society.
2. Teach the fundamental principles of how our country operates at the federal, state, and local levels.
3. Teach students how to solve problems in their community through the political process.

"I think I can get to these kids," I said to Carol with genuine optimism. "It's amazing to think that I could make a difference in their worldviews." She smiled and gave me a peck on the cheek.

And then, while Carol got ready for bed, my inner Energizer Bunny took over.

I decided to draw up an MOU, too. An MOU is a memorandum of understanding, which is a document that lies somewhere on the continuum between a gentleman's agreement and a binding contract. An MOU charts out strategies and goals that all consenting parties agree to pursue. I had always used MOUs at my companies, and they had proven effective in helping me and my employees understand our roles. I thought an MOU would be a great way to tell my Mount Pleasant students that I had high expectations of them, and that they should expect the same from me.

The pact came to me as fast as I could work the keyboard:

> All writing assignments must be typed, double-spaced, and use a 12-point font.
>
> No talking when I'm talking.
>
> No late work accepted.
>
> I commit to each of you that I will do my very best to make this class fun, informative, and worth your time.

Each student was to sign his or her own MOU, and get a parent to sign, too.

A few days later I sat across from Wald and Purcell in Wald's empty social sciences classroom. They reviewed my work: the mission statement, a corresponding semester-long lesson plan, and the MOU.

"Very comprehensive, Steve," said Purcell, smiling, as he paged through the lesson plan. "Field trips, speakers, debates."

"Be careful not to assign too much homework out of the book," added Wald. "They start losing interest fast."

Wald got to the MOU first. His eyes moved quickly across the paper. He turned the page and smirked.

"A memorandum of understanding?" he asked. Wald flipped back to the first page of the MOU, and scanned a few lines again.

"No talking when I'm talking? Parent signatures?" he continued. "The students haven't seen anything like this. The response could be shrugs, no signatures, and excuses. Lines like, 'The dog ate my MOU.'"

Wald and I were developing a rapport, and I knew he was half-joking and appreciated my optimism. But his comment stung. It reminded me that I remained a foreigner on this campus.

I stood up for myself.

"I think the MOU is worth a shot," I said. "It worked with my employees."

"Let's see how it plays out," Purcell said, gathering up all the pages. "You never know how the students will respond."

When I was a kid, I wouldn't have hesitated to sign an MOU. Similar to some of my young peers, I was comfortable with myself at an early age. But unlike my schools' star athletes or homecoming queens, I didn't gain my confidence via some group of admirers. Everyone, after all, wants to be friends with the high-school quarterback. Being a self-assured nerd is different.

I was a very content nerd. I loved math and science, I was compulsive about systematizing, and I had an urge to explore the unknown. In other words, I wanted things to work as they should, and yet I was always wondering if they couldn't work even better.

So I went to Radio Shack. A lot. I was a fourth-grader, regularly pedaling my bike through Houston's swampy summertime air to the local mall. The ride from my house was easy. Meyerland, the southwest Houston neighborhood where we lived, was green, flat, and friendly, and I lived close to the shopping center's ice cream parlor and that glorious, cluttered electronics store. I loved everything about Radio Shack. The circuit kits, tiny capacitors and resistors, the endless selection of switches and knobs—each of those little packaged pieces had a purpose. Put them at your fingertips and, to my mind, the potential was infinite.

A project that sputtered was just as exciting. I'd get to play detective, and go back to the Shack looking for answers. Sometimes I went with friends, although I'd often go alone. I didn't mind when it was just the merchandise and me.

I remember successfully installing a doorknob alarm—touch the knob and a sensor detected contact—for my own room. I also recall some loud buzzer from a circuit kit going off unexpectedly in the middle of the night, which was an indication that I wasn't quite yet an electronics wizard. The racket woke up and angered my dad. But because I was the youngest of the four Poizner kids, he cut me some slack. Actually, it was more like he was middle-aged, a little burned-out on parenting, and somewhat numb to my antics.

He did, however, influence me. My father, Erwin, was a lone-wolf scientist with tremendous passion for his work as a geologist on an endless search for oil. He and my mom were Jews from the Midwest raising a family in oil-happy Houston in the 1960s and 1970s, although my dad wasn't tied to any of the area's many petroleum companies. Instead he was a self-employed petroleum geologist, a quiet and hardworking entrepreneur who had set up a one-man shop in Texas.

My dad was a data geek, too, though of a different sort than you'd find nowadays. I'd visit his office in a downtown Houston skyscraper and enter a world of maps. They were unusual, subterranean maps filled with the squiggly lines of reflected seismic waves traveling through different types of rock. Occasionally he'd hand me a few of these maps to keep me entertained. I was a pig in mud. I'd take his giant magnifying glass and look at all the pale blue ink curving this way and that, as if on a big treasure hunt.

When my dad followed those lines he was searching for a different prize. His objective was to end up on the phone to landowners and oil companies, aiming to bring the parties together because he'd spotted some irregularity in the squiggles that suggested the presence of oil. The chances of finding a gusher were lousy. No better, really, than turning some technology start-up into the next Microsoft. Nonetheless, I would inherit my dad's tolerance and enthusiasm for taking chances as much as his passion for research and exploration. He proved to me that all those qualities could be fulfilling. And that they could keep a family of six in a solid middle-class existence.

If my father was the stereotypical, behind-the-scenes provider, my mom was the outspoken motivator. Standing not much taller than Carol, my mother, Pearl, was eight feet of energy compressed into a diminutive frame. The oldest of four girls, all of them college graduates, Mom made her kids' education a huge priority.

She thought studying was cool. Jerry, Howard, Sharon, and little Stephen—my mom made sure that we kids made our studies, be it for a Bar Mitzvah or school finals, a higher priority than being with friends or just hanging out. We were all quiet, instilled with a midwestern work ethic, and self-assured without being showy. Our four-bedroom, one-story, suburban-style home was largely drama-free, at least until one of us made an academic misstep.

"What is this?" my mother said one day when I had come home with a note from a teacher at Lovett Elementary. It was a Friday and my mom was in the kitchen, cooking spaghetti for dinner, like she did every Friday. There was an Albert Einstein biography and a Hebrew language textbook on the kitchen counter. My mom was a part-time Hebrew teacher and a full-time admirer of the legendary scientist.

"I was talking to a classmate," I said shakily. "We were talking about school stuff, and I didn't get to finish before the teacher asked me to quiet down. But I kept going. I had more to say."

My mom gave me one of her trademark disapproving stares. On those rare but unforgettable occasions, her dull blue eyes could've burned holes into walls.

"No Little League next week, or playing outside," she said, with her hands on her hips. "You'll come straight home from school and go to your room."

To be fair, my mom usually doled out pep talks instead of punishment. She pushed me to get great grades and become involved in school activities. She was so proud when, in junior high, I became president of the laser club, and blueprinted and built a functioning laser. It never occurred to her that laser club presidents were considered hopelessly dorky by lots of their pubescent peers. She just beamed at the sight of my laser beam.

If my mom wasn't worried about my geekiness, then neither was I. She encouraged my curiosity to the point that she'd even shrug off an occasional science experiment gone awry. My mother didn't love it when my homemade smoke bomb once set a next-door neighbor's front door on fire. But she refused to dent the spirit of her little scientist.

"You can be anything you want, Stephen," my mother would tell me when I'd get home from high school. We'd eat kumquats from our backyard trees at the breakfast table, and I'd explain my budding political views. I thought competition was healthy, and I supported free enterprise and individual responsibility.

The TV show *Family Ties* was still a decade off, but I could have been the prototype for Alex P. Keaton. Keaton, the character played by Michael J. Fox, was the conservative son of liberal parents—the sitcom family's lone Republican. True, Keaton wasn't a Jew from Texas. Sharon and my brothers, however, enjoyed airing the fact that I was out of step with a household of Democrats. The gentle abuse could've made me feel like an outsider in my own home, but my mom made sure that I was fine with who I was.

"That's okay, Stephen," she would say. "If you want to be a great businessman, then that's what you should become."

More and more, my mother's can-do attitude became mine. When Sharon returned home from college one Christmas break, I remember her debating over where to apply to graduate school. I asked her if she'd already gotten the paperwork from the Harvard School of Public Health.

"I hadn't even considered it," she said. "I'd never get into Harvard."

"Shouldn't you try?" I asked. "It'll cost you the price of the application fee," I said, doing my best Pearl Poizner imitation. My sister eventually got into Harvard.

But my mom's zeal for me to strive for great things could venture into the irrational. After my sophomore year of high school, she pulled me aside and told me that she was suffering from a fatal disease. She was worried about my dad having to cope with the pressures of both her sickness and raising me, and therefore she had a dying wish: Could I graduate from high school in three years instead of four? My mom wanted me free and clear of a potentially heavy situation.

The request was a head trip. I was a fifteen-year-old kid. My mother—my biggest fan—was dying? Shooing me out the door? Disconnecting me from my classmates and friends? My dad, always the stoic, didn't have much to say.

Nonetheless, this was the woman who insisted that near impossible challenges could be conquered. I was going to prove her right. During my sophomore year, I mapped out what had to be done. I'd attend summer school, apply early to college, and take a huge load of classes in my junior and potentially last year of high school.

I put my head down, fell out of touch with my friends, and kept my mom's odd wish a secret. There was a lot of homework, a sense of empowerment, and great loneliness. I was no longer just an egghead existing on the fringe of the high school mainstream. I was experiencing high school like nobody else. I graduated from Houston's Bellaire High with a 3.9 grade point average in three years.

My mother ended up surviving what was ultimately identified as thyroid cancer. She'd live for decades to come.

I'll never forget the summer after graduation, waving to my parents from the Greyhound bus destined for Austin. I'd soon be attending the University of Texas.

The moment was bittersweet. A year of my childhood was gone, erased in a flurry of accelerated learning. On the other hand, I'd gotten a taste of what it was like to be on the periphery, and I had survived. Plus I'd thrived on the weird challenge that my mother had posed. She loved me, and had made the best decision she could.

As the bus pulled away, my mom cried. My parents, in their own very unusual way, had empowered me.

As schools go, Mount Pleasant's bleakness wasn't completely foreign to me. I remember Jester Center, a then five-year-old, city-block-sized dormitory complex at the University of Texas, having all the soul of a Soviet-style tenement. Jester's rooms were claustrophobic and dingy, and its ugly furniture was bolted down. The three thousand or so students who lived in the twin-building structure regularly flocked to the exits for sunlight. It was a place full of dark corners, where an independent but introverted and particularly young UT freshman could have easily disappeared.

But soon after arriving at the dorm late in the summer of 1974, that dank dungeon came to symbolize a great rite of passage for me. I lived at Jester while receiving an unparalleled education, academically and socially. The University of Texas provided me with one degree in electrical engineering—and another in how to fit in.

Shortly after arriving at Jester, I met one of the dorm's residential advisers. He was a gregarious guy and, at that point in my life, I was not. He fished a lot out of me. I told him that I studied hard. I liked sports okay, but I was no Longhorns linebacker. As a kid, I got beat up by a kid named John, who was the bully in my Houston neighborhood. I'd belonged to a few academically oriented school clubs. Did I mention that I enjoyed studying?

"Have I got the group for you," he said to me one day while the two of us ate hamburgers in Jester's cafeteria. He had a smile so big that it shifted his cheeks up and to the sides, like they had to make way for an overabundance of joy.

"A bunch of students who like to do all sorts of community projects," he added. "They're bright and studious people, too."

I knew more about making smoke bombs than helping old ladies across the street. Still, I liked the idea of mixing with people who were smart and applying themselves. I wanted to have lots of friends at UT. I figured that I'd better try to find some common ground.

Many of the approximately 250 members of the school's coed Alpha Phi Omega fraternity, I soon discovered, were a tad square. Alpha Phi wasn't a traditional Greek frat. It was a service fraternity, founded on the principles of the Boy Scouts.

Well, I wasn't completely unlike the frat's brothers and sisters, and

I appreciated that the members of Alpha Phi were friendly, supportive, and energetic. I quickly realized that I could apply my smarts to
help organize and plan community-based projects as effectively as I
used them to ace a calculus test. I worked my way into the higher
ranks of Alpha Phi, enjoying every step.

We organized blood drives instead of beery benders, raised
money for local charities, and ran campus clean-up projects. We
were in charge of the Texas flag that was trotted out for many football games, too. It was huge, about sixty-six by one hundred twenty
feet, and you didn't want to be the fraternity member who blew the
choreography involved in running it out onto the field. Fumbling the
state flag is about as big a Texas faux pas as stepping on a cowboy's
new Justin boots.

I ended up serving as president of the fraternity, and through the
group met lots of people involved in other student activities, too. They
opened doors for me to join various organizations on campus.

Among other things, as an upperclassman I became head of UT's
Ideas and Issues Committee. It was a fancy name for the person
charged with securing and scheduling speakers for talks on campus, which wasn't an obvious role for me. I hadn't been groomed for
life around a stage. I'd been no great shakes on my high school debate team.

So I summoned the words of my football coach of a mother: *You
can do whatever you want.*

I aimed high, inviting everyone I could imagine to come speak,
including the day's biggest names in politics, business, and entertainment. What did I have to lose?

At my request, people like Henry Kissinger, Lily Tomlin, and Dan
Rather all spoke on the UT campus. Their acceptances to my invita-
tions emboldened me to ask myself what else I might someday ac-

complish. I began to think that if I put myself out there and tried new things, I could be more than just a bookworm or a Boy Scout.

Of course, the speakers inspired me, too. Henry Kissinger, despite the audience's heckling for his role in the Vietnam War, was charismatic and unflappable. Dan Rather was articulate and clearheaded. Hunter S. Thompson, I can undoubtedly say, was a growing experience.

Scheduled to speak on an early-spring evening, the outlandish and hard-partying writer told me not to bother picking him up at the airport. He'd have a friend get him to the campus.

Thompson lived up to his crazy reputation, showing up an hour late for his appearance—smashed. A huge audience was waiting. We had to lie him down on a conference table backstage, and pry a bottle of Wild Turkey out of his hand. He then proceeded to pass out.

When he came to, I gathered myself.

"Mr. Thompson, you're going to do this, aren't you?" I asked, standing over him.

Who was I but some punk college kid prodding a pop culture icon? I'd never even read anything by Hunter S. Thompson. But I had to get a speaker to the podium.

"Give me a sec," he said, adjusting his sunglasses. "This'll work out."

In a few minutes Thompson got up. He blew off any pretense of delivering a speech. Instead he walked onstage, fielded questions for thirty minutes, and left to a lot of applause. I breathed a giant sigh of relief.

My academics at UT were not secondary. I could still play student with the best of my peers, often holing up in Jester and the nearby Perry-Castañeda Library, studying for my degree in electrical engineering.

The classes weren't easy. I worked very hard, for instance, at a

course called Feedback Loops. A feedback loop is an electronic circuit capable of making midcourse corrections, like re-aiming a rocket
that's moving off its designated path. I wrestled with algorithms and
enormous math equations, and sometimes asked myself why I went
to all the trouble. I'd known from early in my college career that the
gold ring I really sought was launching technology businesses. Did I
need Feedback Loops?

I did. The class gave me background knowledge in engineering
and, just as significantly, perspective that would one day serve me
well as a Silicon Valley entrepreneur. Being an entrepreneur isn't unlike existing inside a feedback loop: After my schooling, I'd find that
there would be many moments, at Strategic Mapping and SnapTrack,
where I regularly had to rethink my approaches to products, markets,
and strategies. Really, the best entrepreneurs, I'd learn, are those who
repeatedly make successful midcourse corrections.

But I was still years away from SnapTrack, and a few months shy
of getting my college diploma, when I received an honor during
halftime of a November 1977 University of Texas football game.
Administrators at the forty-thousand-student school recognized
me as the college's top male undergraduate student of the year. The
award came for my academic achievements as well as my extracurricular leadership. Knowing what a wallflower I'd been when I arrived on the campus, I was proudest of how I had adapted to my
college environment. But I'd also nailed my studies. I graduated in
the spring of 1978 with a 3.96 GPA, and was singled out as one of
the top electrical engineering students in the nation. I had been accepted into business schools at Harvard, the University of Chicago,
and Stanford.

And then, just like that, I was another face in the crowd. At Stanford, I had to start the assimilation process all over again. The irony,

however, was that becoming a member in good standing of the Stanford Graduate School of Business required none of the social talents that I'd developed in college at UT.

At Stanford I questioned—for the first time in my life—if I was smart enough to make it. Every day, I slogged through classes like cost accounting and linear programming with about three hundred very serious classmates. Making matters worse, I was one of the school's youngest students, and a lot of my peers came with intimidating East Coast or California pedigrees. The majority of people in my class had already enjoyed professional success. Many came from families deeply involved in business. Some of the students regularly wore white, pressed, and monogrammed button-down shirts to school.

I dressed in T-shirts and tennis shoes, and would have to work off my graduate school loans for a decade. Over the next two years, I became much more intimate with Stanford's libraries—like the Meyer and the Jackson—than with California's surf or beautiful hills. I visited nearby Lake Tahoe only once.

I joined an eating club, but that was so I wouldn't have to spend time cooking meals. John Elway, who played quarterback as an undergraduate at Stanford before becoming an NFL superstar, ate at the same club. I kept my mind on passing classes. The hulking Elway, I bet, also had to focus a whole lot on passing.

While I received a fantastic education at Stanford, honestly what I remember best was reaching the finish line. Only when I lifted my head for graduation in the spring of 1980 did I feel like I truly belonged. I'd gotten through all my work, and then some: I graduated in the top 10 percent of my class. It was a huge honor and achievement, considering that some of my classmates would become Silicon Valley legends.

As for me, the business school graduate who would eventually become a Silicon Valley dropout? I'd do what plenty of dropouts do: return to school. It would take me twenty-plus years, and the challenges would be nothing like those that I had faced in Houston, Austin, or Palo Alto. But the feelings in my own Mount Pleasant classroom would be all too familiar. I'd be a freshman again, figuring out exactly how to fit in.

CHAPTER 4

Will the Kids Buy It?

They trudged into the classroom on a cold, overcast morning in early January 2003. Tall and short, male and female, primped and disheveled. They were the thirty-two Mount Pleasant seniors arriving for day one of my American Government class. The kids settled behind the desks of classroom 612, which was usually Wald's domain. There was an exchange of nods and pleasantries— I'd subbed in front of some of these students before. Then they all quieted down and looked up at me with one collective game face.

Showtime.

"Welcome to an important semester on American government," I said, slowly walking the center aisle that bisected the arranged desks. "As you approach graduation—and the age of eighteen—you're inching ever closer to becoming an adult citizen of this country." I tapped a finger on a couple of desks as I strode. "According to the United States Constitution, you'll soon be awarded many rights and obligations.

You'll increasingly want to know, as the Declaration of Independence puts it, about 'Life, Liberty, and the pursuit of Happiness.'"

Nobody so much as nodded. I went on.

"Every school day for the next five months we're going to analyze lots of questions together. What makes the American system of government so great that millions of people risk their lives to come to this country? How can you solve seemingly unsolvable problems by working through the American political process?"

Someone dropped a few books on the floor. Maybe on purpose. I didn't break stride.

"Are your rights as an adult any different than they were as a student?" I paused, for dramatic effect.

"Should the death penalty be legal?" I asked. "What options do you have if the police stop you?"

And then the big line of my opening monologue: "Why do we even *need* government?"

It was a tough crowd. Nobody shifted to the edge of their seats, let alone gave me an ovation. Still, my inner voice told me to stay the course. I told myself that I'd already had an unresponsive audience as a substitute teacher. Everything worked out before, and it would work out again.

But this was different. I was no longer a pinch hitter teaching here and there. This was my class, and I had to think about the arc of spending an entire semester with these students. Would they stay engaged? Would I make the class too hard? Too easy? Could the kids and I respect and trust one another? Would they like me? Would I like them?

Off the bat, I wanted to sell them on my curriculum and myself. So I conjured visions of being an entrepreneur again: I was pitching a concept to thirty-two kids who weren't altogether unlike venture capitalists. As was often the case with potential investors, the students had short attention spans. Winning over both audiences required crisp message delivery. I had to appear motivated, too. An audience that isn't necessarily swayed by the details of a pitch can still be captured with passion. Those first investors in SnapTrack, I recalled, had little idea of what the company would produce (neither did I). They were hooked by my enthusiasm.

"I'm telling you, this can be a totally fascinating semester," I said, passing out copies of the course highlights and the memorandum of understanding. "I promise that I'll give you all the energy I have to make American Government a fantastic class."

I was not obligated to make any vows or pledges to the kids. It's not like I needed the students to write me checks to float a new company. On the contrary: Technically speaking, I was the gatekeeper. My thirty-two kids needed to survive twelfth-grade government to graduate. Within reason, I could make them jump through whatever hoops I held up, because without my seal of approval—as in, giving out passing grades—failing students would at the very least be held out of the summer's graduation ceremonies, where all of their friends and peers would be moving on in life.

Yet I felt nothing like a gatekeeper. I saw myself as a steward. I'd been empowered by Purcell, Wald, and the state of California to enhance these kids' lives. I wanted to help shape my students' futures, to raise their awareness of the potential opportunities available to them. My highest hope was that they'd feel like they could each make a difference.

Thirty-seven minutes into the opening class, however, the students' notions of twelfth-grade government weren't nearly that romantic. They had no visions of my class unfolding like some triumphant scene from *Stand and Deliver,* or another one of those high school feel-good movies.

"What's a memorandum?" said a girl while brushing her blond-streaked hair. "Why do I need to get my mom or dad to sign it?"

"It's an agreement that we're both going to try to make this class totally worthwhile," I said. "We use memorandums of understanding all the time in business. I wanted you and your parents to know that I'm committed to this class. Hopefully, you will be, too."

The girl tapped her brush against her books. She seemed annoyed.

"My dad says your business made you something like a billionaire," interjected a roundish boy with gelled hair. "How big is your house?"

"It's comfortable. I'm lucky to live in a nice place," I said, leaning against the desk.

"What's your name?" I continued.

"Pete Franco," he said. Pete had fuzzy, thick eyebrows and a goofy grin. "I guess I'm lucky enough to go to school here. Or would that be unlucky?"

I decided it was time we all got to know one another.

"Why don't we go around the room and introduce ourselves," I suggested, crossing my arms. "I'll start," I added, and gave a brief description of myself, and my time spent in the Silicon Valley and Washington, D.C.

"Antonio Boras," said the boy next to Pete. "I'm lucky enough to sit next to Pete."

There was laughter.

"I guess we'll keep it to names for now," I said. At least I could count on my experience as a CEO to help me keep the kids reined in.

There was Joe Reardon, Tracy Cardenas, Chad Cortez, and Audrey Valverde. There was Donny Mates, Komal Saldanha, Alan Wilson, and Jill Sullivan.

"Jimmy," said another kid, who was squat and imposing. In spite of the cool winter weather, the boy wore a white tank top, and his arms were muscular and cut. His face was a continuous grimace, from his creased brow to lips seemingly unable to turn upward. His head was clean-shaven.

"What's your last name, Jimmy?" I asked. There was enough silence for the moment to feel awkward.

"Vega," he said, looking straight at me.

I turned away. We weren't through with one class and I'd already entered into some kind of uneasy face-off.

"Let's keep going," I finally said, and after introductions I explained what the students might expect in terms of work over the course of the semester. "Your grades will depend on more than your quiz and test scores. You'll have to complete a community project, and I'll also count class participation and writing assignments. It's important for your future that you're able to write down your thoughts and opinions," I said.

"Writing in a government class?" said Komal Saldanha, blowing a stray strand of hair out of her eyes. "Is there a lot? We've already got writing in, like, *writing* classes."

This wasn't proceeding as I had hoped. Couldn't the kids see that I was looking out for their interests? They weren't exactly taking to me, or to my agenda.

A jolting buzzer sound crackled over the loudspeaker on the wall. That was Mount Pleasant's "bell." The period was over. Some of the kids hopped out of their seats as if their desks were on fire. Once the classroom emptied, I shut the door behind me and slowly walked into the lounge for lunch.

"Is California on the verge of becoming a red state?" quipped Delaney, who was already eating.

"No," I said, walking right by the empty seat next to him. "For the record, I'm aspiring to leave political bias at the classroom door."

I decided to lower my odds of entering into a conversation with Delaney. I sat down next to Wald at the other end of the gathering.

"They weren't interested in hearing much about my plans," I said. "It didn't matter how I tried to package them."

I took a bite of my turkey sandwich, and reflected on the class. "And this one guy, Jimmy?" I continued. "I thought he was going to punch me when I said there would be writing assignments. Are they just second-semester seniors wanting to slide out of here, nice and easy? Do they have *senioritis*?"

"Yeah, they're eager to get out," said Wald, opening a bottle of water. "But in a way you're lucky."

"How's that?" I asked.

"The kids you've got have already endured three and a half years of high school. They can picture the diplomas in their hands," he added. "You want nightmarish students, kids that don't care? Teach freshmen. They think about dropping out every other week."

Wald took a couple of sips of water before putting the bottle on the table.

"In this place, your kids are counted as the ones who still have hopes that they're going to make something of their lives," he added. "Relatively speaking? You've got the ambitious ones."

I struggled to spot such ambition during my first week of teaching American Government. I needed to lay some groundwork around the concept of democracy, and the students displayed little enthusiasm for my lectures. I could only hope that my initial, underwhelmed feelings for them weren't showing. Displaying disappointment isn't a great idea when your job is to lead a classroom full of kids toward a brighter future.

"In the history of the world, the formation of American democracy was new. It was a different type of government. One might think of it as the world's biggest start-up," I lectured to the class four days into the semester. "Democracy was an unconventional kind of idea for a government, sort of like selling pet food or beauty supplies on the Internet may be a novel idea for a business.

"Why might a new government succeed or fail?" I asked. "I have a hint for you. The answers aren't that different from why an online pet food business might fail. Why might that kind of company not survive?" I asked.

Nobody raised a hand.

"What would happen if the president of the pet food business stopped overseeing the business, and the customers didn't get the services they'd expected? For instance, what if they didn't receive the delivery of products they'd ordered online? What if one of the company's employees was treated unfairly?"

Still no show of hands.

"Anyone?" I said, trying to hide the exasperation in my voice.

The fifth period class wasn't over until 12:34 P.M., and it was only six minutes after noon. I was determined to get some answers.

"Would you want to live in a country where the leader didn't want to lead?" I asked. "If the money issued by the government wasn't any good, or people were treated unfairly? Do you think that's when a government might fail?"

I was answering my own questions, and still not generating discussion.

"Tracy," I said. "Would you want to grow up in a place where the government wouldn't let you have a job because, I don't know, you wear glasses?"

Tracy Cardenas struck me as one of the brighter kids. In introductory surveys that the students had already filled out, she was one of the few to write responses in proper and crisp sentences. But my question caught her by surprise. She was slumped in her desk chair.

"No, that'd be a terrible place," she said reflexively, crossing her leg and picking at the shoelace of her Nike sneaker.

I waited to hear more from her. After a few seconds of silence, however, I determined that she'd finished.

"We'll come back to Tracy later," I said.

"And what if the government instead let only people who wear glasses have jobs?" I continued. "Would that be fair?"

Nobody spoke up. I felt like I was talking to a wall.

I walked to the center of the room and crossed my arms.

"Does anyone remember the one term in the reading assignment from last night that might bring people of different opinions, like those who think only certain groups should get jobs, or get paid, or get their children educated, to agree?" I asked.

Joe Reardon raised his hand. I pointed to him.

"Compromise," he said, without conviction. Joe was a tall, skinny kid, and he was sitting near the wall that displayed a big student-drawn map of the United States. "In a democracy people have to be willing to compromise," he said, his deep but hesitant voice gaining a little momentum. "Not everyone gets what they want all of the time."

"Thanks, Joe," I said. "Nice work. That was great."

His response had been unexpected. Joe was slightly awkward and very lanky, and was the one "special education" student in the class. Purcell had told me that Joe was dyslexic, but not so impaired that he deserved exceptional assistance in my classroom. If Joe requested extra time for his work, I would give him what he needed. So far, he hadn't asked for any additional support.

"Please try to read the textbook a little more closely," I suggested to the class, suppressing the urge to ask if people actually did the reading, which so far had amounted to fifteen pages.

"You'll all benefit from understanding these basic issues before we get into meatier stuff," I said, sitting down heavily into the chair behind Wald's desk. "Plus there's going to be a short quiz tomorrow on chapter one."

I skipped lunch in the lounge that day and came home. The students' indifference had been really frustrating. I needed to catch my breath.

During the thirty-minute drive back to the hills, I debated my ability to have a semester's worth of patience. Fifteen pages of reading over the course of several days—was that so much to ask? Didn't anybody want to say anything? I marveled at the notion, as Wald had put it, that my students could be characterized as "ambitious."

It was a cool but clear afternoon. When I came home, I sat fully clothed on a lounge chair by the pool. Rebecca was at school and Carol wasn't around. My phone rang. It was an old friend from Snap-Track asking if we could get together sometime soon.

"Must be nice sitting by your pool on a Thursday afternoon," he said.

"I wanted some fresh air. Not a great day as a teacher," I replied. "I'm telling you, I already notice a big difference between substitute teaching a few classes and overseeing students for the long haul. Sort of like the difference between babysitting and having your own kids. I can't just shrug at their flaws and hand them off, knowing that they're ultimately someone else's responsibility."

"So what are these kids like?" he asked.

"They're pretty unmotivated," I said. "It's hard to get them to read a dozen pages."

"Not like SnapTrack," I added. "Do you know how fun it was to manage a company full of really smart, inspired people? You feel like you can accomplish anything. Total rush."

"Like driving a sports car," he said. "But you opted to drive a school bus instead. Different vehicle."

We made a date to get together for dinner. I hung up and thought about what he'd said: driving a school bus. He was right. If I didn't recalibrate my expectations, we would all be in for a very long semester.

I stared at the swimming pool, watching the pool sweep lazily make its way across the water's surface. During my Silicon Valley career, I took pride in my ability to manage all sorts of people. The Valley is full of eccentrics, and I tried hard to listen to their needs. I found that some of my employees worked too much, others had to be barricaded in their offices to get anything done, while still others had to have someone standing over them—day or night—in order to write programming code. I'd learned to become tolerant of lots of different personality types, because I knew that in return I'd get my workers to be productive. At the end of the day, they wanted to generate results, too. We'd all come to the Silicon Valley to make our mark.

But now, as my friend had said, I was overseeing a completely different group of individuals. From an intellectual standpoint, I absolutely knew not to expect Silicon Valley–caliber ambition and smarts from East San Jose schoolkids. Yet emotionally, I grappled with the students' unresponsiveness to nearly any question I posed. The differences weren't only in our expectations or zip codes. They were in our wiring. Getting the best out of my Mount Pleasant students, and giving them a great education in the process, would be a huge management challenge.

The next day, Purcell stopped me in the hall before class. He was about to tie me up into more knots.

"Got a moment?" he asked.

"One of your kids switched out of the class," he said, closing the door to his office behind me. "It was Chad Cortez. He came in and told me that he didn't want to continue. Thought the class might be too hard."

"Wow. That's disappointing," I said. "Any way he'd reconsider? There's a lot of good stuff to come."

Purcell waved his hand.

"Stay the course. It's okay to challenge your kids. In fact, it's great. Maybe Chad doesn't want to do any work, and he thinks you'll flunk him faster than another teacher. Let it go."

It was time for class. Walking across the campus, I couldn't shake Purcell's news. Could I satisfy my urges to challenge these students without alienating them? Were they all ultimately going to end up in Purcell's office requesting transfers?

I walked into room 612, and the students looked stoic. One more thought occurred to me before I pulled out the quizzes and distributed them: I'd been fired. For the first time in my life, I'd been told that I wasn't doing my job sufficiently. And the person who'd humbled me with the decision was a kid from the rough side of the tracks.

Honestly, plenty of my students could've made an argument for firing me. Not because of poor job performance—at least not yet. But the kids could've accused me of surprising them with a workload that was as alien as it was challenging. Decades' worth of bureaucratic public education policy in the Golden State had often left Californians expecting to be underwhelmed by their state's schools. My demands for community projects, public speaking, and a lot of writing were going to make for a highly atypical semester of twelfth-grade American Government.

Students from the 1950s and 1960s might have found me to be less foreign. Back then, California's public education system was considered one of the nation's most dynamic—even labeled "utopian." Local communities funded the schools in their areas with property taxes, and schoolteachers had the ability to create and tailor lesson plans to the needs of their particular kids. Often teachers set the bar high. California produced waves of accomplished students. Lots of those kids also had the good fortune to enter into the state's highly regarded public colleges and universities. Altogether, this educational process helped California seed itself with some of the nation's best and brightest young people.

But then an unassuming yet persistent social worker from East Los Angeles named John Serrano questioned the state's century-old approach to funding its schools. In the late 1960s, Serrano was pulled aside by an elementary school principal, who urged Serrano to move to a wealthier community within the Los Angeles Unified School District. The move, said the principal, would get Serrano's bright little boy the great education he deserved, because schools in more well-to-do communities were better funded.

Serrano followed the principal's advice. But he couldn't forget the modest school he'd left behind. Serrano himself had come from humble beginnings: His mom was a seamstress, and his dad was a shoemaker. Why weren't all California students benefiting equally from the state's public education policies? Just how much disparity existed across the state in the quality of a public school education?

A hard look at the system turned up large inequalities among schools. Financially, the state's wealthy neighborhoods were generating more money from property taxes than its poorer neighborhoods were, despite the less affluent neighborhoods getting taxed at higher rates. Among communities, differences in annual per-student funds ranged wildly: Some public school budgets had twice what others did for their students. Reduced funds meant compromised resources for learning, in terms of fewer enrichment classes, underpaid teachers, and overcrowded classrooms. In the end, there was wide belief among education experts that kids in California's low-income areas received inferior educations to those living in affluent neighborhoods.

In 1968, Serrano put his name on a class-action lawsuit. *Serrano v. Priest*—at the time a woman named Ivy Baker Priest was California's state treasurer—challenged how public schools were financed. The case ultimately brought about radical change.

Too bad that change wasn't unquestionably for the better. Victory by the Serrano camp triggered what has become an increasing centralization and bureaucratization of California's public education system. The Serrano lawsuit's most obvious effect: Half of the state's education monies now come from California's general fund, so that schools in poor neighborhoods receive approximately the same basic funding per pupil as schools in wealthier neighborhoods. Sounds good on paper, until you realize that the state legislature—which isn't terribly qualified to run California's schools—does exactly that. Too often, the results of such centralized management have been negative.

California teachers in kindergarten through twelfth grade classrooms frequently feel powerless, like puppets manipulated by the state's Department of Education. After all, it's bureaucrats in Sacramento determining what students read, study, and see on their tests, whether those kids are rich or poor, first-generation Americans or fourth-, or if they hail from the state's northernmost reaches or southern border. Teachers hoping to keep a classroom full of diverse students interested are often in for an uphill battle, because their lesson plans have to address demands established by people who are, in more ways than one, very removed from the kids. But debating such issues means wading into California's ridiculously bloated education code. A code, by the way, that takes up several large volumes.

The bureaucratization of the state's education hasn't done much to improve the performance of California's students, either. There's still a pronounced achievement gap between schools in poor and rich neighborhoods. The latter often receive more parental support, as well as more motivated students. Set in a lower-income environment, Mount Pleasant, for example, continues to underachieve. In 2008, its kids collectively led the school to score nearly 20 percent below the state goal in a widely used California education metric called the Academic Performance Index, or API. The picture isn't entirely rosy in supposedly better school districts, either: Nowadays only 38 percent of California public schools' white students—for whom English is presumably a first language—read at nationally competitive levels. An argument can be made that California's attempts to overhaul education has caused all boats to sink instead of rise.

So it was predictable that my students didn't know what to make of my unusual, pumped-up lesson plan, which their other teachers had neither the time nor the resources to brew up. The kids were dubious for weeks. Debates? Visiting politicians? And what about all those writing assignments? Outside of their English classes, my students had never seen so many writing assignments. Why couldn't I just stick to lectures on topics like Congress and civil rights?

One Friday in mid-January, the students turned in what was assigned as a two-page essay about the life of an immigrant living in the United States. From a standpoint of logistics, I knew that the paper might not be too challenging. Many of the kids likely had potential interview subjects living with them at home.

I flipped through some of the papers while the students watched a brief video. I vividly remember the quality of work I received.

Tracy Cardenas, the girl with the quick wit and the polished writing, gave me two complete pages of typewritten work. She wrote:

My grandmother came to the United States from Mexico. She moved because her brother had emigrated five years earlier. He'd told her that there was good work in America, and a better life. But she had to spend the first five years in California working as a maid.

Then I glanced at Joe Reardon's homework. He gave me a page and a half. I saw, along with the effects of his dyslexia, real effort:

I have a friend who have an uncle came from El Salvador. He say he was leaving a very dangerous place. Hopefully, he said, safer existence to America.

I flipped through the pile twice, and couldn't find any work from Pete Franco. There was, however, something from that tough kid— Jimmy Vega. Jimmy hadn't once spoken in class without me calling on him first, and his responses were usually halting and without much substance. I didn't know if the boy was in a gang, but he sure looked the part. Jimmy usually appeared angry, with his chin slightly raised and his dark eyes seemingly stuck at half-mast. He also had a long, raised scar on his right forearm.

He wrote:

My cousin came from Chiapas. He likes America alot. He has to work hardd but dosnt make much money. He wishes life coud be better. Still he'd move again if he lived somewere else.

The video that the kids were watching soon ended, and shortly afterward the bell buzzed over the classroom's loudspeaker.

"I want to see Pete Franco and Jimmy Vega, please," I announced over the din of shuffling papers and zipping backpacks.

I sat down at Wald's desk. As the classroom emptied, the two boys approached me.

"What's up, Mr. Poizner?" said Pete.

"I couldn't find your homework in the pile," I said, sitting back in my chair. "Did you turn it in?"

"No. No, I didn't," he said in a very relaxed manner. Pete always looked at ease and happy, kind of like a talk-show host. He had the pleasant voice to go with the demeanor. "I didn't get around to it," he said. "Sorry."

"Pete, these assignments aren't optional. You have to do them," I said. He nodded while maintaining a grin. "I expect you to do this homework over the weekend."

Pete agreed to write the paper and then turned to catch up with his friends.

"Hey, Mr. Poizner," said Jimmy, stepping toward the desk. He was wearing a black San Francisco Giants sweatshirt.

"Hi, Jimmy," I said, adjusting my glasses. His bald head gleamed in the fluorescent light.

"I saw your homework and just wondered if you'd felt that it was complete."

"Yeah," he said with a twist of his head, like he was trying to loosen up some of his thick neck muscles. "It's the immigrant paper."

"The assignment was for two pages, Jimmy," I said. "This is only a few sentences."

"I did what you said. I talked to an immigrant and wrote some stuff down," he said in a nasally, subdued voice, as if he were pushing the words through a broken nose.

"I think you can do better," I said. "I bet there's more to your cousin's story."

"Probably is, yeah." Jimmy's hands were on his waist. The muscles around his skull moved when he talked.

"But I don't want to do more," he said. "This isn't a writing class. This is government. I don't want to do more writing. You know? I mean, why?"

"Jimmy, the writing helps you to understand the information and organize your thoughts," I said, leaning my forearms on the desk, which brought me awfully close to him. "It's important that you be able to think clearly, not just for my class but for all your classes. Really, for whatever you attempt in life."

"Mr. Poizner, I don't want to do more writing," he replied with a shrug. "I just don't."

We looked at each other for a few seconds. It felt like minutes. I was at a loss. He refused to do more work? What if I insisted? Was he going to hit me?

"Maybe give it some more thought. I'll see you Monday morning," I said.

Jimmy gave his neck one more twist. Then he turned and walked out of the room.

I needed to assemble more than sentences and paragraphs with the kids. I needed to build trust. Getting them to have faith in me, I thought, would encourage the students, and make them more open to the work I wanted them to do. Maybe I could even get a kid like Jimmy to really understand that I wanted very good things for him. Unfortunately, in a tough public high school like Mount Pleasant, faith is in short supply.

One didn't have to look far at Mount Pleasant to see why kids might feel dubious about school and those in charge of it. Student bathrooms were dilapidated. Security officers patrolled the campus, watching the kids from golf carts. Classes were held in shoddy temporary buildings. Currently as many as 18 percent of all California public school classes are taught in temporary buildings, which are really thinly veiled trailers. What kind of a message do these regrettable images send to students? In the kids' minds, how much do school administrators care?

Teacher turnover is another big problem in creating trust. The endless parade of new faces that kids encounter—as I mentioned earlier, nearly one out of two inner-city California public school teachers quits within five years—means the constant rebuilding of student-teacher relationships. Imagine if you were married and had to meet a new set of in-laws each and every Thanksgiving: Will these people be easygoing? Funny? Serious? Mean? The students have to get to know complete strangers on a regular basis. Whether they like them or not, they're usually stuck with them.

Sometimes turnover is extreme. Half a dozen years before I arrived at Mount Pleasant, California's elementary schools endured such a dire teacher shortage that some schools hired faculties that were 50 percent new. The students of those schools must have felt as uncertain as if they'd moved to another town.

In fact, parade enough new teachers in front of students and they'll revolt. The author and longtime teacher Jonathan Kozol, whose critically acclaimed books about public education include *Death at an Early Age,* tells a story about his once taking over a class (not in California) that had seen twelve teachers in the same academic year before he was handed the chalk and erasers. The kids had become so angry and distrustful of Kozol's predecessors that on one occasion they'd locked an instructor out of the room during class. The teacher "banged on the door and shouted warnings to the children," writes

Kozol in *Letters to a Young Teacher*, "but they wouldn't let him in."
When another teacher finally rescued him, he was "red in the face,
and stamping his feet like Rumpelstiltskin."

I knew that I was contributing to this revolving-door dynamic.
Starting off the semester by wearing pressed pants and shirts did
nothing to help me fit in with either the denim-loving students or the
other teachers. And the guest-teaching businessmen who had preceded me at Mount Pleasant had set lousy precedents. There was the
one whom Wald had entrusted but had appeared only once or twice in
front of a class. When he did teach, his lectures were filled with jar-
gon. Another businessman had made millions in real estate and liked
to brag about his accomplishments. The students could have easily
wondered: Was this Poizner dude going to bail on us? Or get bored?
Or start bragging? If he's here for only a semester, will he even care?

I thought that my memorandum of understanding would, with re-
gards to trust as much as to work expectations, help the kids believe
in me at least a little bit. "Do not hesitate to ask for extra help," I'd
written in the memorandum. "Feel free to contact me, including at
night and over the weekend." I'd listed my personal e-mail address
and phone number.

But the Monday after my face-off with Jimmy, I was still waiting
for the last MOUs to be returned.

Settled into their desks for class, I reminded the students that the
MOU was more than a formality. "These memorandums are counted
in your grades," I said. "I still need completed MOUs from Komal Saldanha, Pete Franco, and Chad Cortez."

There were a few snickers from the ranks. I forgot that Cortez had
fired me.

"You'll have it tomorrow," said Pete. "It's at home, in a pile somewhere. It's signed. I just need to remember to bring it in."

"Please don't forget," I said. "What about you, Komal?"

Komal was a bright light in the classroom. Ponytailed and energetic, she was one of the few students who'd already emerged and
semiregularly volunteered opinions. Just the week before I'd had to
stop her from going on and on about Fourth Amendment issues. She
had said how important it was for her fellow students to know that
the Constitution protected people from being arrested or searched
without authorities first having probable cause. She also spoke at
length about liberties and privacy, and had even made a crack about
how she wished the Fourth Amendment applied in her own home,
where her father was forever bursting into her room and telling her
that reading and homework were for sissies. The disclosure had
thrown me.

"My dad doesn't know about signing the MOU," Komal said. "I
mean, he's already told me that I probably won't finish out the school
year here. We may move back east, and then I wouldn't be getting my
diploma at Mount Pleasant anyway. So maybe I can just skip the
MOU . . ."

"Let's talk about it after class, Komal," I interrupted, and then transitioned into the day's lesson.

But Komal's comments persisted in my thoughts. It's one thing to
know that as a teacher at a substandard public high school you're undoubtedly going to face kids who come from broken or unstable
homes. It's another to witness defeat or dispiritedness firsthand. I was
saddened at the prospect of someone as lively as Komal enduring a
shaky home life.

What father wants to demoralize his own child the way Komal's
dad was apparently discouraging her? I imagined that no parent—
not even Komal's—would purposely inflict such damage. Maybe her
dad was depressed. Perhaps he never graduated from high school

and didn't know the significance of getting through all of one's classes, putting on gowns with your friends, or grabbing that diploma in June.

My personal experiences were so removed. I'd been very lucky. The Poizner residence in Texas bore some resemblance to Ozzie and Harriet's house. My dad moved us into Houston's Meyerland neighborhood because it was kid-friendly, and my parents were determined to get us solid public school educations. Dinner at our house was on the table at six P.M. every night. Most Sundays we'd go to Baskin-Robbins for ice cream. There were gifts at Hanukkah, and family trips.

Carol and I have always been there for Rebecca, too. For years Carol chauffeured Rebecca to all her softball games, and nowadays she orders Rebecca tickets for Fall Out Boy concerts the minute they're available. Carol's huge family showers Rebecca with attention and love, too. We both make sure that Rebecca does her homework, and my mother would be proud to know that I'm unrelenting in my demand for good grades. Okay—when it comes to schoolwork, Rebecca doesn't like me so much. But she respects me, and knows that I care. When I take her to a Saturday movie and we later hit the sundae bar at Fresh Choice, I'll often hear music to my ears: "Dad, this is awesome," she'll say, fountain spoon in hand. "What are we doing next weekend?"

On a Tuesday around my third week of teaching American Government at Mount Pleasant, I realized that the personal tragedies facing some of my students would be far outside my realm of experience. Building connections and trust over the course of a semester was going to be difficult. For some of these kids, the whole world was unsafe.

Class ended, and a gum-smacking, hardened student named Benita Johnson approached my desk.

"Hi, Benita," I said. "How's it going?"

"Mr. Poizner, I won't be in class again until next Monday," she said. Benita wore a lot of makeup and eyeliner that only made her pale blue eyes look colder.

"My fiancé just got caught for driving a getaway car in a bank robbery," she said. "I have to help him deal with a bunch of things."

Later I'd look in a local newspaper. There it was, a story about arrests made in connection with an attempted bank heist. Benita probably wasn't inventing a way to skip class—at least not on that day. She had likely been telling me the dreadful truth.

I didn't see her for the rest of the week.

Robert Wald listened to me retell the tale Benita Johnson had told me minutes earlier. I worried aloud that I might never relate to these kids. He didn't flinch.

"Steve, the farther up into the hills you go, the nicer the homes, and all the stereotypes about people and achievement that go along with those nicer homes," he said, grabbing a Ping-Pong paddle and readying for Ian Ellison's serve during a lunchtime pickup game in the lounge. "Some of these kids have predictable East San Jose lives. Just because you've been put in a classroom together doesn't mean you're suddenly on the same wavelength."

"I'm just amazed at the strikes against them before they even open a book," I said. "You kind of wonder if they'll ever really wrap their heads around schoolwork."

Wald and Ellison played a few points of Ping-Pong with zest, like they didn't have a care in the world. Ellison was a mellow guy originally from the nearby surf Mecca of Santa Cruz. Besides being a teacher, he helped coach Mount Pleasant's football team.

Wald was born and raised in the Silicon Valley. He and his schoolteacher wife were thrilled with their ten-month-old baby boy and seemed content with the unpretentious existence they'd carved out for themselves. Wald wasn't hung up with his lot in life, nor was he preoccupied with the tough hands dealt to some of Mount Pleasant's students. He no doubt wanted those students to succeed. But he wasn't afraid to flunk the kids who deserved to fail.

"How do I put this, Steve?" said Wald, who was having his way with Ellison, hitting the ball to one corner, then another. "There's the suffering at home, and that might be bad and to be avoided or soothed," he said. Ellison hit the ball into the net.

"The question is, can your students recognize that there's good suffering, too, for something worthwhile?" Wald asked, spinning the paddle in his hand while waiting for Ellison's next serve. "Like the suffering involved in getting a strong education."

Wald pinpointed the source of the tension that had been building inside me over the first three weeks of the semester. I had wanted my students to immediately recognize my worth and the value of Poizner-style suffering.

All at once, I wanted to be the teacher who had the unorthodox but perfect plan! The new teacher everyone could trust! The teacher who wouldn't have to hear the apathy or pleas for sympathy that every other teacher at Mount Pleasant hears. In other words, I was impatient, just as I had been at twenty-six, when I was convinced that I already knew my way in another world—the world of the successful Silicon Valley entrepreneur.

I left school that day repeating a reassurance to myself. I said that, despite our differences, the kids would buy into me, as a teacher and a person, over time. I just needed to have faith in my lesson plan, and in my ability to teach it.

Plus, I had to avoid getting caught up in the students' feelings, and my own. I'd never taken events too personally while captaining SnapTrack, and I told myself that I should take on that same mindset at Mount Pleasant. However, as the semester wore on, I'd find that the business of teaching was more emotional than the business of business.

A couple of days later, I believed that I was about to win over the kids with my curriculum. Temporarily win them over, anyway. In just twenty-four hours, we would have our first guest speaker.

Similar to the volunteer work I'd done at the University of Texas twenty-five years earlier, I'd already made call after call to line up interesting speakers who could help inspire my Mount Pleasant students, and bring some civics-related topics to life. My standing in Silicon Valley and experience as a White House Fellow helped me pull some strings. I'd lined up lots of great people for the semester: newspaper reporters, scholars, politicians, attorneys, people for and against the legalization of marijuana, and Pentagon VIPs.

I thought that the speakers would trigger the students to ask questions and generate dialogue. My biggest hope, of course, was that these guests would inspire the kids to think hard about the topics being discussed, and the kinds of opportunities that the world could offer them.

"Tomorrow an agent from the Federal Bureau of Investigation's San Francisco division will come speak to us," I said to the class on a cold, rainy day in the last week of January. "Can anyone tell me what the FBI does?" I asked.

"Shoots criminals," announced Komal.

"It does investigate crime," I said. "It's also an intelligence agency looking for people who want to undermine our government. For example, the FBI tries to locate terrorists before they perform horrible acts.

"The agent's name is Michael Gimbel, and he's making a special effort to visit us," I said. "I want you to come up with some thought-provoking questions for him to answer. Here are some ideas: Why might the FBI care about the Silicon Valley? What might the FBI want to help protect around here? What in San Jose might interest terrorists?"

The next day, Gimbel arrived right on time. Dressed in a gray suit and looking every bit the professional, he discussed the FBI's duties for about twenty-five minutes, speaking to the class as well as to Purcell, who had taken a desk at the back of the room. Unlike me, Gimbel kept everyone spellbound with his cloak-and-dagger tales.

After he finished, I led a round of enthusiastic applause for Gimbel. Then I opened up the floor to questions.

"What do you guys have to ask Mr. Gimbel?" I said. Nobody raised a hand.

"Who remembers some of the ideas we talked about yesterday?" I asked.

The silence continued. This was getting old. But I couldn't take the lack of response personally. Maybe the kids had stage fright. They'd participate when they were ready, I said to myself. I hoped that they'd be ready soon.

Finally happy-go-lucky Pete Franco raised his hand.

"Pete," I said, pointing to him.

"Can you spin your car like the cops do on television?" he asked Gimbel. "Kind of, uh, do a one-eighty?"

I swallowed hard and hoped my face wasn't turning red with humiliation.

But Gimbel politely responded, and when the school bell sounded he gave the students some FBI souvenirs before leaving. Purcell pulled me aside on his way toward the door.

"Maybe you should rethink the students' preparation for the speakers," he said. "You're getting there. I don't know if there's ever been a cop on this campus for a reason other than to keep the peace. Good work."

A couple of the kids were having a mock-shootout on their way out of the classroom, pretending that their new FBI highlighter pens were guns.

At least the students had all been interested. My next task was to turn entertainment into education.

CHAPTER 5

Killer Material

I told them to watch TV. It was Monday morning, and I instructed my students to go home the next night—Tuesday, January 28— and turn on their televisions. They were to watch George W. Bush deliver his State of the Union address for two reasons: The president would tell the kids about current issues facing the nation, and Bush would be proposing an idea that he and I—yes, Steve Poizner—had discussed. In other words, I told them, we'd talked about something that was important enough to make prime-time television.

"Almost nobody knows about this, either," I explained, standing in a corner of the classroom, looking confident with my hands on my waist. "You could say it's a national secret."

Room 612 became uncommonly quiet. I could imagine the thoughts popping into the kids' heads: Watch TV? National secret? Were we still in Poizner's class?

"Wow!" said Tracy, her incredulous smile revealing dimples in her cheeks. "This is the kind of homework I like."

"My dad never turns off ESPN," said Komal, her head shaking fast enough to send her ponytail whipping around behind her. Then she stopped. "I wonder if he'd make an exception."

"Come on, Mr. Poizner," said Pete, slowly kicking off one of his big Timberland hiking boots to pull up a loose sock. "You don't know what the president is gonna say. You just want our attention."

Pete was half right. I did want the kids' attention. In the days following Gimbel's presentation, the students were full of questions about the FBI. They were riveted by his war stories (perhaps they had clammed up because he was a bigwig). Well, I had great tales from my days as a White House Fellow. I could drop names—from Condoleezza Rice to Osama bin Laden. To borrow a phrase from the many comedians I've enjoyed seeing live—and I've watched plenty of them, even at my own wedding—I had "killer material" for grabbing my small student audience. It was time to use it.

"No, I'm not fooling with you," I said to Pete, crossing my arms and leaning against the wall. "I know exactly what Bush will say. Not only that, I persuaded him to say it. When the two of us last met."

"Dude, no way," said Tracy, hooking her hair behind her ears, as if that would help her hear every word I'd utter. "You met President Bush?"

"Do you want to hear the story?" I asked. Many of the kids nodded. "It all started when I became a White House Fellow . . ."

I launched into an explanation of the White House Fellows program, which began in 1964 when President Lyndon Johnson decided to allow fifteen Americans to spend a year working directly with top White House staff.

"Like what Monica Lewinsky did?" asked Komal.

"No, she was a White House *intern*. That's different," I said. "And please don't interrupt."

The program was designed, I went on at some length, to groom these chosen few people to become community leaders.

"In 2001," I explained, "I was lucky enough to be selected for the program. I lived and worked in Washington, D.C., with eleven other Fellows from September of that year to August 2002 . . ."

I performed a quick visual sweep of the classroom—and realized that I was losing them. I wasn't wowing the crowd like Jerry Seinfeld, or even FBI agent Michael Gimbel.

Komal was fiddling with an earring that she'd taken out of her ear. Pete passed a note to another kid. Joe, the overachieving dyslexic student who waited on just about every word I said, was glassy-eyed.

"What about the president?" Tracy said impatiently. "What's he like? When did you guys talk about the stuff that he'll bring up in his speech?"

I quickly weighed my options. I could continue with the narrative line I was following, and take the chance that a few kids in the class would care about the process and possibility of becoming a White House Fellow. I mean, I'd found the whole White House Fellows experience incredible, and I wanted to inspire the kids. Or I could dive right into a discussion about meeting the most powerful man in the world, and squeeze in some information about the presidency and the role played by the U.S. government's executive branch. Maybe the latter was all I could ask for my kids to absorb.

I went with option two.

The president, I explained, is a very busy man who has to wear lots of hats. Among other things, he's commander-in-chief, meaning he's in charge of the military. He's the chief diplomat, which means he's our country's leading spokesperson. And he's the chief executive—

the leading decision maker when it comes to the nation's foreign and domestic affairs. I had spent months before I'd met him preparing a report that I hoped might convince him to change some policy in the United States.

"Was he nice?" asked Joe.

Enough background, I thought.

I told the students that I met Bush in the Roosevelt Room, in the West Wing of the White House, on an extremely hot July afternoon in 2002. I sat at a long table with a dozen or so other staff members when the president walked in. He wore a dark suit and had sweat on his forehead. He'd just gotten off a helicopter. We all stood up. Someone brought him a Coke.

"How big was the helicopter?" asked Jimmy.

"I didn't see the helicopter, Jimmy," I said.

I explained to the kids that someone gave a presentation before mine, and that President Bush hated it and barked at his assistants. He seemed really irritable. I was freaked out! My big chance to pitch a program to the president of the United States, and he was in a bad mood.

Someone handed Bush my nine-page report about chronic problems facing poor teenage kids. Then he looked at me, his eyes peering over his small reading glasses. Before I could say anything, one of his aides informed me that I had about ten minutes to give my presentation. I'd originally been promised a half hour.

"Mr. President, children and teenagers from underprivileged families face persistent problems," I recalled saying. "They're using a lot of drugs."

"Uh-huh," he'd said, with his unmistakable Texas twang.

"Teen pregnancies aren't going down, and juvenile offenders are committing most of their violent crimes right at the end of the school day," I had said. "The federal response to these problems has been admirable, but fragmented."

The president, I told the students, listened very carefully.

"So what do you propose we do?" President Bush had finally asked me. He no longer seemed mad.

"We should enter more kids into mentoring relationships," I'd explained to him. Bush had nodded, and I'd gone on with the statistics to support my argument, and what I'd thought was the best approach to creating successful programs. When I had finished, he smiled.

"Good work," the president had told me. "Let's keep going on this. I'd like us to develop some executive orders."

That, I explained to the kids, was my huge moment with the president, and a small but real example of government at work.

"When you watch the State of the Union address tomorrow night," I said to the students, "listen for Bush's proposal to reapportion hundreds of millions of government dollars for mentoring programs for kids."

My students thought about the story for a minute. Then the reviews came in.

"He really paid attention to you," said Komal, "even with all the other junk he has to think about."

"That's cool, Mr. Poizner," said Pete. "What did you guys do after that? Did you get his autograph, or shake his hand? Did you get a high five?"

"You don't high-five the president, dummy," said another kid. "Come on!"

I told Pete that it wasn't the right situation for a high five, and that the president left soon after my presentation. But I did say that it was a huge honor to speak to the president as a member of a team that was briefing him on volunteerism and domestic policy issues. I was thrilled that he'd taken my suggestions so seriously.

However, I didn't feel the need to tell the students that I was, in essence, practicing at Mount Pleasant what I'd been preaching about mentoring to President Bush only the year before. I couldn't envision much to be gained by asking the kids to reflect on the fact that I had proposed aid for students exactly like them: challenged youth who could frequently use more role models. Likewise, I didn't bother boring them with the details that, as a White House Fellow, I'd contacted many of the nation's mentoring experts, gathering convincing research about how disadvantaged kids in quality relationships with adults were far less likely to start using drugs or alcohol. There was no reason to go into the minutiae of how I'd found more than one hundred existing federal mentoring programs and suggested that the programs would be a lot more effective if they were coordinated.

I left those many details out. All that mattered was that my students listened to my lecture and got a glimpse of how good ideas might be processed and popularized at the highest level of government. I'd successfully laced my American Government lesson with killer material. Soon the bell sounded.

Two days later, Joe Reardon walked into class with a big smile on his face.

"Mr. Poizner, you were right. President Bush talked about the proposal exactly like you described it. My mom and dad watched, too," he said, rotating his backpack off his shoulder and sliding into his seat. "It's awesome to know that you made a difference. Seeing the president talk about your idea makes me understand that, you know, government gets decided by people."

Never before had my homework assignments reaped such satisfying rewards.

· · ·

My White House intel got plenty of play in Mount Pleasant's social sciences lounge, too. "Fun to watch, Steve. Like having a backstage pass," said Wald at lunch, just after I'd spent my entire Wednesday government class answering enthusiastic questions about Bush's speech. Ellison patted my back. Delaney approached me, nodding.

"Always difficult to listen to that guy. I can't believe you subjected your kids to so much W," he said, dropping his brown-bagged meal onto a seat with a torn cushion. "But it was great to hear about your work. How did you present it to Bush?"

I sat down and ate lunch next to Delaney, and we enjoyed a surprisingly amicable conversation that drifted from one aspect of politics to the next. He told me about the many, many years he's put in supporting California politicians. He'd also worked with the local teachers' union and was always watching out for the little guy.

"I don't like the idea of businesses exploiting the system to the detriment of the many," he said.

"You know, Simon, I have a populist streak in me," I said, wiping my mouth with a napkin. "I'm always thinking about the masses, the little guys, in terms of making sure that they don't get a raw deal from some corporate monolith. Those giant companies were often my competition in Silicon Valley, and I don't like any business getting so big that it's verging on a monopoly. I don't want options taken away from people."

"Maybe we agree on a few things," said Delaney, crossing one leg over the other and wrapping his hands behind his head. "But if you ran for office I could never support you. You're just the wrong party. That's a fact."

I had a sinking feeling that Delaney was poised to take a swipe at me. How many seconds would pass before he launched into the usual anticonservative conspiracy and bile for all things Republican?

But it didn't happen. For one day, anyway, Delaney was too intrigued by my time in the White House, and my play on national television (so to speak), to completely alienate me.

"So who did you get to meet while you were a White House Fellow?" he said. "Did you travel?"

I told him that one of the best parts of the Fellows program was
the regular lunches we had with some of the biggest names in politics
and Washington, D.C. About three times a week, the dozen Fellows
sat down for lunch with one VIP after another. Condoleezza Rice, Supreme Court Justice Antonin Scalia, and Ben Bradlee from *The Washington Post*—it was a Who's Who of American power and politics. We
got to bring up anything that came to mind.

"What I wouldn't do for fifteen minutes with Condi Rice," said
Delaney.

I explained that the Fellows traveled a lot. We went to China and
Vietnam as representatives of the White House to discuss Sino-U.S.
relations. I found that we were taken very seriously—Fellows were perceived as an up-and-coming wave of American influencers. (I'm quite
proud to say that former White House Fellows include generals Colin
Powell and Wesley Clark, Pulitzer Prize–winning author Doris Kearns
Goodwin, as well as high-level judges and state politicians.) We had
eye-opening meetings with U.S. ambassadors and the vice premier of
China, who wanted to talk with us at length about Shanghai's eco-
nomic development. In Hanoi we discussed the improved plight of
workers in developing countries, and were given factory tours. Our
hosts showed us respect in an odd way, too: We Fellows were important enough that some of our hotel rooms were likely bugged.

Delaney listened closely to my recollections. Then he smiled a real
smile.

"I have a request. I'm wondering if you'd come talk to one of my classes about some of your White House experiences. Maybe hit some points about how one becomes a Fellow," he said. "You could plant a seed with my students," he said. "You never know what will happen."

I was happy to get the offer and quickly accepted.

As I pushed my chair away from the lounge table, I thought to myself that maybe Delaney was extending an olive branch. Perhaps, I thought, my visit to his class will get our relationship over some invisible hump. Wouldn't it be nice not to brace for Delaney's outbursts every time I set foot in the lounge? My killer material was opening doors for me.

Two weeks later, I stood in front of Delaney's twelfth-grade English honors class.

"For those of you who don't know him, this is Mr. Steve Poizner," Delaney said to his class, standing off to the side and gesturing toward me with his right arm. "Mr. Poizner is a guest teacher this semester, teaching a twelfth-grade American Government class in Mr. Wald's classroom. He's a Republican and a former Silicon Valley entrepreneur . . ."

Did he need to mention that I was a Republican?

Delaney continued. "Last year, Mr. Poizner worked in the White House, serving under President Bush's Republican administration . . ."

Does he have to polarize us at every turn? I said to myself. The olive branch was sprouting thorns.

"Mr. Poizner," Delaney added, "was recently a White House Fellow. The Fellows program is open to people who have already spent some time in a profession and are interested in learning about leadership from high-ranking members of government. We're lucky to have Mr. Poizner here to tell us about his experiences." Then he gave me the floor.

Fortunately, Delaney's strange introduction was the only awkward moment of the period. I told the kids that anyone with enough desire could consider becoming a White House Fellow. Among the members of my group, which had included soldiers, lawyers, and emergency room doctors in their thirties, I was an oddity—a forty-four-year-old entrepreneur.

"Most guys my age and in my line of work," I said to the class, "want to start more businesses, or buy an island and retire. I think my wife would've been happy if I'd just bought the island. But I'm kind of different."

Delaney's kids were quiet and attentive. I hadn't been in a Mount Pleasant honors class in a while. It was fantastic. I'd forgotten how well behaved, interested, and articulate Mount Pleasant's students could be.

They peppered me with questions. I explained that the White House Fellows program gets as many as two thousand applicants in a year, and you have to go through sixteen grueling interviews held in different parts of the country before landing a spot.

"What was the hardest question you were asked?" said one girl. "What was your reply?"

"One interviewer gave me this fictional scenario where the earth's civilization had been destroyed by nuclear war and that it would be up to three people to rebuild society. The three people, the interviewer said, could be from any time in history. Right then and there, I had to choose those people," I explained.

"I picked Ben Franklin, Thomas Jefferson, and Albert Einstein. To me, that trio had the right blend of leadership, intellect, and wisdom. Then one of the panelists asked me, 'What, no woman?' and I realized my oversight," I said.

The girl who'd asked me the question broke into a righteous grin.

"I thought for a second before making a request to change my response so that I could include the poet Emily Dickinson," I said.

"Why her?" said the same girl.

"Her poetry still gets taught. At least it did when I was in school," I said.

The kids laughed.

"I remember that her work remained unconventional, even though it was about a century old. She was an independent thinker who's still influential in modern times. Somehow that satisfied my interviewer," I said.

The students asked more questions about the screening process. I lost myself in the conversation.

"An interviewer also requested that I show my artistic side—just to knock me a little off balance. She told me to get up and sing or dance or draw something on the chalkboard that was in the room," I said. "At first, I was a little panicked. My daughter won't get near a dance floor with me. Plus I have a terrible voice. So I drew stick figures of my wife, daughter, and dog with chalk. All I can say is that question must not have been worth many points."

Delaney's class laughed again. I was surprised when the bell buzzed over the room's loudspeaker. The period had gone by so quickly. The kids gave me a round of applause, and Delaney offered me an enthusiastic handshake.

I left his classroom and walked through one of Mount Pleasant's atriums. Over the noise of student shouts and laughter, clashing feelings ricocheted around inside my head. There was Delaney's curious behavior. Hates me, likes me, hates me, likes me. Why did I even care? Because I crossed paths with the guy virtually every day? Because his dislike for me was illogical, and I put so much stock in logic? I resigned myself to the fact that he and I would never be in sync.

I also struggled with the notion that I'd had more fun teaching Delaney's class that one time than I'd ever had teaching my own class.

It's not that I couldn't share war stories with my kids. They enjoyed many of them. But Delaney's honors students were more sophisticated and ambitious. They didn't listen to me because I sounded like the narrator of some sort of White House Fellows highlight film. They seemed genuinely interested in the program, as if it were not out of the realm of possibility that they might one day apply. The truth was, I connected with Delaney's honor students better than I connected with my own.

I didn't share every crazy tale from Washington, D.C., with my Mount Pleasant audiences. There were some memories from that time that were undoubtedly gripping, but more life-and-death than inspiring. They often involved the two people closest to me: Carol and Rebecca.

I first got wind of the White House Fellows program while I was still working at Qualcomm. I immediately bounced it off my family.

"What would you guys think about moving to Washington, D.C., for a year?" I asked Carol and Rebecca after coming home one night from the Qualcomm offices. Eight-year-old Rebecca was sitting at the dining room table, sighing while she looked over her math homework—multiplication. Carol was nearby in the kitchen, cooking chicken and rice for dinner.

Carol let out a "now what's up his sleeve?" groan. I briefly explained the Fellows program to the two of them.

"There can be as many as two thousand applicants," I said as Carol spooned out the rice. "About a dozen get accepted."

"Heaven forbid you try something easy," Carol said. "You know how close I am to my family," she continued, handing a plate to Rebecca. "They're all local. Rebecca is in a good school here."

"It'd be an adventure. It's only a year. Then we'd return to the house and to Rebecca's school, no problem," I said, grabbing three sets of

silverware and winking at Rebecca. She winked back. "It's a great platform for launching into public service, and it's an interesting city," I
added. "The Smithsonian, the White House, the Lincoln Memorial.
Getting to know the nation's capital would be great."

We sat down for dinner at the counter between the kitchen and
the living room. We'd moved into this house in the hills from my old
condo—the condo where I had started my career as an entrepreneur in
1983—in 1997. Now it was a few years later, and the place still needed
furniture. The roof and landscaping had been redone, but we'd limped
along with a sparse collection of ancient and ratty La-Z-Boy seating.
Predictably, my work had meant more to me than furniture shopping.
Carol had been lobbying for a while that we do something about the
empty expanse.

Then she had an epiphany.

"What if we bought a house in Washington, D.C., big enough for
my family to come stay with us, and they'd come out for visits?" she
said, her eyes gazing across the living room area. "We could furnish
that place with this house in mind. When we move back, we'd sell the
D.C. house and take our furniture home with us. Then this house
would feel complete."

Carol had taken us from having one house without furniture to
two homes—plus the services of an interior decorator—in no time
flat. Now I had to think about the whole endeavor.

Ultimately I'd come over to Carol's way of thinking. She'd had a
good idea.

I applied to become a White House Fellow in February 2001. Four
months later, Carol and I both had our reasons for celebrating when I
discovered that I'd made the cut. The yearlong fellowship would begin
the following September.

Everything went according to plan. I should say almost everything.

We purchased a home in D.C., complete with extra rooms for guests. Rebecca was accepted at a respected private school.

Before beginning the fellowship on September 4, 2001, each Fellow had already been given a work assignment, which would shape a significant part of the year's upcoming demands and White House experience. I could've been assigned to a number of positions—in the Office of Science and Technology Policy, the Office of Management and Budget, the Department of the Treasury, or elsewhere. Instead, White House staffer Richard Clarke picked me to work under him, with the National Security Council. (I'd work on domestic policy, specifically the mentoring program, toward the end of my fellowship.) Clarke was a veteran who had served in the White House, largely in leading roles addressing security and antiterrorism, since Ronald Reagan had been president. I'd be doing serious work.

"Your experience with emergency-response technology could be invaluable," Clarke said to me in my first week on the job. His watery brown eyes, perfectly enunciated words, and pale complexion belied his ample confidence and swashbuckling toughness. "Hope you're ready to roll up your sleeves," he added. Little did Clarke or I know how hard we'd soon be working, or how often we'd be broaching the topic of emergency response.

Early on the morning of September 11, I was on a small, chartered bus with the other White House Fellows, headed out of town for a two-day planning retreat in northern Virginia. Carol reached me first, from her cell phone. She was at a Krispy Kreme with her brother and his girlfriend, who were visiting from the Bay Area. It was her brother's birthday. The three of them were on their way to Mount Vernon. They were minutes from the Pentagon.

"Did you hear? A plane flew into one of the World Trade Center towers," she said.

I hadn't heard. None of the other Fellows had heard yet, either. Howard Zucker, a Fellow and a physician from just outside of Manhattan, subsequently called his parents. They could see the New York City skyline from their home.

"My mom says a second plane just flew into the Twin Towers," he said, shaking his head. Zucker was sitting next to me on the bus. He looked at me with an ashen face. "Steve, I have a bad feeling that these crashes aren't accidents."

The group of Fellows arrived at the retreat facility and crowded around a single television. Soon we were all caught in an avalanche of numbness, despair, and sadness that had instantly rumbled across the nation. Another plane had crashed into a Pennsylvania field, and a fourth had been flown right into the Pentagon.

So close to that Krispy Kreme. So breathtakingly scary.

The phone lines were soon tied up. All I could do was hope that my family was okay. We Fellows quickly learned that Washington, D.C., had transformed. Tanks were lumbering through the streets, fighter jets went zipping overhead, and armed soldiers were standing guard in the subways.

We called off the retreat. In the seven hours it took me to get home, I finally understood why Carol, with the health problems she has endured for decades, treasures every day of her life. Mere survival, I thought, on the traffic-clogged trip back into the D.C. metro area, was a gift. Nonetheless, I didn't want my nation to suffer any more than it already had, either.

Corny as this might sound, I'll flatly admit that in the days following 9/11, I knew there was no place I'd rather have been than serving my country. Clarke personally took me aside and asked if I wanted to be reassigned to a different White House Fellows job that would take me far away from the White House. He believed that the White House would be an ongoing target. I said that I was staying put.

But Washington was undoubtedly a grim place during that fall and winter. I felt horrible for my wife and daughter. I'd brought them there. Nobody in their right mind would have visited us; our home's guest rooms stayed depressingly empty. The threat on our lives, meanwhile, felt real and constant. The post office that handled our mail limped through an anthrax scare—we'd go days without deliveries, and our mailman confessed to us that he was on anti-anthrax medication. A gunman fired on customers at a gas station that we'd frequented. One night shortly after September 11, some nut left me a voice mail message on my office phone.

"Steve Poizner, I'm going to kill you!" a gravelly, heavily accented voice had said. "Blow up your car! Shoot your head!"

The Secret Service ultimately analyzed the call for me, which they said came from somewhere in Europe. The agents didn't feel the threat was serious enough to offer me special protection. Meanwhile, I'd convinced myself that the call was from some crank that somehow got my name and number. What else could I do? I wouldn't tell Carol and Rebecca about the incident until we'd left Washington and returned to California.

Maybe two weeks after September 11, Clarke called me into his office. He introduced me to a Secret Service agent, who proceeded to open a small, gym-style bag. Inside was a garment that looked something like coveralls—a one-piece, protective suit designed to be worn over regular clothes. But these coveralls weren't meant for the service workers you might find in clean rooms or Jiffy Lubes. The outfit was a biohazard suit. There was also a gas mask.

"You need to get fast at putting this thing on," the agent had said. "In an emergency, you'll want to be in it, with the suit all closed up, in thirty seconds. Take it with you everywhere you go."

That night I brought the suit home. Carol got upset. I didn't blame her.

Clarke had given me only one suit, and there was no way I would ever put it on in a situation where Carol's and Rebecca's lives were also endangered. I didn't want to survive some horrible terrorist attack only to have the two of them perish. So no, I didn't take the suit everywhere. It just sat in its gym bag in my office.

"What does the destruction of two huge buildings in New York City have to do with the United States Constitution?" I asked my class one Friday in late February. The State of the Union address had come and gone nearly a month earlier. But I still tied some of my White House Fellows anecdotes to the class curriculum. I figured that the kids could learn a few things in my lesson plan by connecting the dots between, say, the 9/11 attacks, the Fourth Amendment to the United States Constitution, and life in East San Jose.

"Imagine this scene in Washington, D.C. It's a week after the September eleventh terrorist attacks," I said to them, pacing my usual path, which bisected the room's three dozen desks. "One of the city airports remains closed, inconveniencing thousands of people and leaving lots of workers jobless. There's still a huge military presence around town, and the coast guard is roaming the Potomac River, protecting the city's shores. Over in Manhattan, remains of the two World Trade Center buildings continue to burn, and there isn't yet a plan in place to clean up the mess.

"What do you think the people of those two cities were feeling?" I continued. "Were they scared? Depressed? Ready to move away?"

"If something like that happened here?" responded Tracy, crossing her arms. "I'd be totally frightened. I wouldn't want to leave town, but I'd say do anything to make sure those plane crashes don't happen again."

"How about you, Komal?" I asked. "Would you feel the same? Would you want the government to do whatever it could to protect you?"

"Heck yeah," she said, stopping the pencil she'd been twirling on her desk. "I'd support the government however to feel safe."

"Jimmy?" I said.

Jimmy Vega, running his fingers over his smooth head, shrugged and gave me a glare. Even after seven weeks of teaching, I still found him unsettling. Were he and his thug friends soon going to push me up against a wall?

I looked elsewhere for a response.

"Joe, what do you think? Could there be a problem with giving the government more power in the hope of reducing the chances of a terrorist attack?"

"There was something about that in the reading for today, right?" said Joe, looking up toward the ceiling. He seemed reluctant to continue. Maybe he was afraid that he'd appear foolish if he said the wrong thing.

"You're on the right track," I said, trying to tease more out of him. I really liked Joe. He was interested in the subject matter and frequently raised his hand to speak. He came to me outside of class for extra help. His dyslexia hampered the quality of his work—but I was already prepared to give him an A for effort.

"I think it was something about preventing the government from actually being too powerful," he added.

"You're getting warmer . . ." I said.

Reardon gave me a blank stare. I decided not to push.

"Remember—we've touched on this before, but now we're going to dig deeper. The Fourth Amendment?" I asked.

I continued. "The Fourth Amendment involves the principle of limited government," I said. "That government can't just do whatever it wants, even if its leaders think they know what's best for the people. The government can do only what the people have given it the power to do.

"After the 9/11 terrorists attacks," I added, "the highest-ranking officials in the United States government wanted to find the people responsible for the crimes. But it wasn't easy, and not just because they couldn't quickly locate the criminals. The politicians and military leaders were struggling with the idea of listening to certain people's phone conversations or reading their e-mails, simply because these people were thought to be suspicious. Under the Fourth Amendment to the Constitution, Americans are protected against such actions."

I went on a little more. "The Fourth Amendment is why a San Jose police officer can't stop and frisk you just because he feels like it. The Constitution prevents the government from making excessive judgments and assumptions. See how the laws that protect you might also affect an entire nation?"

"Hasn't always protected some of my friends," Jimmy muttered.

"After 9/11," I said, "U.S. officials were debating how much they could spy on people without violating their rights."

"How do you know so much about all this?" Pete asked.

"Because I was with the nation's leaders when they were deciding what to do after the terrorist attacks," I said. "We were in a building that was about as secure as Fort Knox."

Fort Knox—that got the students sitting up in their seats.

"What did the building look like?" Pete asked.

"Were there guns everywhere?" said Jimmy.

I told the kids what I could about my often-classified experiences with Richard Clarke, and my workdays inside Clarke's tightly sealed, third-story offices in the 120-year-old, European-style Eisenhower Executive Office Building.

The Eisenhower building is right next to the White House's West Wing, which houses the Oval Office. Clarke, who was George W. Bush's counterterrorism chief until he retired in 2003, had a suite of offices in the Eisenhower building. I needed a high-level security clearance just to enter the building, and Secret Service agents frisked me daily. I couldn't bring my cell phone into Clarke's office because, among other reasons, its telephone service wasn't "secured." In addition, access to Clarke's office—which was formally known as the Office of Transnational Threats—was possible only by first passing through a door that looked like it came off a bank safe. It was massive, with a dial-type locking knob in the middle.

I worked with a couple of dozen other people in the office. I was the lone technology geek, but that made me popular. Clarke liked me because I was the person he could turn to for answers concerning emergency communications systems and the potential for terrorism to spread via the Internet.

"My coworkers were definitely way different from me," I told the students. "These guys were G.I. Joe meets James Bond meets Rambo. Veteran soldiers with crazy tales about war and special operations missions performed all over the world."

"Like what?" said Jimmy, who had recently told me, in a rare talkative moment, that he wanted to become a marine after his "release from Mount Pleasant."

"Parachuting into Afghanistan, sneaking up behind enemies, overthrowing dictators. Things like that," I said. "Clarke told me that he himself was on Osama bin Laden's hit list and used to say that he'd been chasing bin Laden on and off for the last twenty years. From one cave to the next."

The class responded with lots of oohs and aahs.

"I can also tell you that I worked with the FBI on protecting the

Internet," I said. "I had discussions with Silicon Valley company presidents about what terrorists might do to us online. I discussed my
findings in meetings with people in the National Security Council.
They were the folks in charge of defending our nation."

"So did you spy on people illegally?" said Komal. "Did you read
their e-mails, like going against what you said is in the Fourth Amendment?"

"All I can tell you, Komal, is that there were many discussions
about such issues at the highest level," I said, looking at my watch.
Class was almost over.

"And there will be plenty of discussions about it on our level, too,"
I said. "Enough tales for today. Don't forget that your papers on government and privacy are due on Monday. You have to give me arguments for and against the authorities having more power over people.
Remember that these are big issues. What you're considering gets debated by big-time politicians in Washington."

I was happy it was Friday. The effects of life at Mount Pleasant—
teaching, grading papers, and preparing a lesson for the next day that
would grab my students—wore me down even more than it had when
I was teaching more classes as a substitute. What strength I'd gained
in terms of familiarity with the routine and a one-hour day of teaching was lost in the demands of the daily grind. Plus I continued to
poke my fingers into other parts of the education pie. I'd gone from
visiting classes at other public schools to helping to develop a local organization whose mission in part was to open more charter schools in
California. Charter schools are publicly funded schools that operate
outside the command of centralized school district decision making.
At the time I became involved, charters were still very experimental

and the organization demanded plenty of my attention. The moon-lighting gig both excited and drained me.

But tonight I was glad to give the education universe a rest. Carol had arranged for her parents to look after Rebecca while the two of us went to San Francisco to meet some friends. We had a date to go see comedy—an entertainer named Will Durst. We loved Durst. We'd seen him many times before.

"Think we'll get there early enough to sit near the front?" I asked as we drove north toward the city. Carol turned down the sports talk show on the radio. Baseball's spring training had begun.

"If we're farther back, it's not the end of the world," she said. "I'm happy if we can hear every joke."

Neither of us ever tires of good comedy. It is, in fact, a cornerstone of our marriage. Carol and I are, in many ways, quite different. I chase achievement, and she pursues family and life experiences. But one of our common denominators is an addiction to a good belly laugh or three.

Way back in 1980, not long after the two of us met at the Palo Alto chapter of the Jaycees, Carol helped me land guest speakers for some of the Jaycees' meetings. We wanted speakers for the same reasons I'd sought them out years earlier at the University of Texas—to educate, entertain, and inspire a crowd (and us). It was as Jaycees that Carol and I asked luminaries like President Carter and Chief Justice Warren Burger to come and talk. We weren't hurt that they turned us down, because we hosted great guests, such as Bill Walsh, who was the San Francisco 49ers head coach, and U.S. Attorney General Dick Thorn-burgh.

But to Carol and me, the top acts were frequently those that made us laugh. Back in 1987, I spearheaded the South Bay Comedy Picnic, a local event that ran for five years and raised tens of thousands of dollars for Stanford Hospital. It took the two of us—and plenty of other Jaycees—more than a year to organize the picnic, which attracted thousands of people and featured more than two dozen comedians. Some were great (like Ellen DeGeneres, Rob Schneider, and our man Will Durst), others more eccentric (like The Amazing Jonathan). We once landed Robin Williams, but it wasn't his finest moment. He tried new material, and he tanked. Recalling an unfunny Robin Williams, however, always keeps a cocktail party conversation rolling.

When Carol and I got married in the Bay Area's Kohl Mansion in 1988, our guests found that our vows practically incorporated a commitment to laugh. Although the reception was outside, there were two reasons to go indoors: One room in the mansion had a hot fudge sundae bar; the other held a stage, and the whole party piled into that room to watch a comedian by the name of Jim Samuels. We thought people might like Jim better than an evening remembered for having too many toasts. Most important: Carol and I had a blast.

Through the years, we've also had stand-up comedians at our house for parties. But our most hyperbolic-comic moment came when I sold SnapTrack and we rented out a huge ballroom to celebrate. We were so grateful for our good fortune, we invited every investor, friend, supporter, and janitor connected to the company. A big event, we thought, deserves big entertainment. And out on the stage came Dana Carvey.

The yuks, however, were harder to come by during my year as a White House Fellow. Rebecca missed her friends, and Carol missed her family. We weren't used to the cold East Coast winters, let alone the siege mentality of a city that had literally been under attack. I had one incredible experience after another, watching oral arguments delivered to the Supreme Court justices, touring New York City's Ground Zero, and meeting deputy secretary generals at the United

Nations headquarters. But I often worked long hours, which was hard on my family. You just don't cut out early when the National Security Council wants a report.

Fortunately, the spring brought more than a thaw. Carol's family flew cross-country to see us, and Rebecca and I gave them tours of the West Wing. After a while, my daughter even became an expert at pointing out all the factual flaws in the iconic painting *Washington Crossing the Delaware*.

Definitely the lightest moment of our year in Washington came on a warm spring night when the three of us had tickets, along with some other White House Fellows, to sit in the Kennedy Center's exclusive president's box. Rebecca, Carol, and I each got our fill of free M&M's. They came in boxes decorated with the presidential seal.

All sugared up, we sat down for a production of *Romeo and Juliet*. But we soon discovered that it was a unique interpretation of the tragedy, complete with Portuguese dialogue and a topless actress. Talk about an unforgettable performance.

The lightness I felt after that night in Washington, D.C., was the same kind I carried home with me many months later, on the other side of the continent, on a February Friday night that included Will Durst, my wife, Carol, and some wonderful humor. The busy week I'd just endured at Mount Pleasant faded rapidly.

And I carried that happiness with me all the way into the next Monday morning. All the way, that is, until I looked up at my American Government class and asked the students for their papers.

CHAPTER 6

Turnaround Strategies Meet the Classroom

Tracy Cardenas's paper on the Fourth Amendment was half-finished. But at least she turned in something. Komal Saldanha didn't give me a paper. Neither did Pete Franco, nor three other students. Jimmy Vega, meanwhile, blew off the class.

I called out the half dozen (present) offenders' names at the end of the period.

"I'm not kidding around," I said to the handful of students, my back against the chair. "You guys have to start doing the assignments. We're two months into the semester. You've got to hold up your end of the bargain."

"Tracy," I said, and pulled out her two pages of work from the stack of papers I'd received. "I gave this a quick read. What you've got is great. You know how to make a point. You have a gift with words. While I read it I was thinking, man, Tracy sure knows how to make an argument. She could be a lawyer someday. But you delivered only half of the assignment. Why didn't you do the rest?"

"I ran out of time, Mr. Poizner," she said, and glanced at her watch. "It was already late last night when I got as far I did. I don't know. I thought it was probably good enough."

"Maybe you should've started earlier," I said. "I want you to finish." I reached out to hand the paper back to her. Tracy lifted her right arm grudgingly, as if it weighed a thousand pounds.

"Komal," I said, turning to see her looking toward her toes. At least Komal appeared a little remorseful. She also kept rubbing the back of her neck with her hand.

"Your contributions in class are really nice," I continued. "You know this stuff inside out and have a lot to say. Why didn't you write the paper?"

"I hate writing, Mr. Poizner," she said, and took a deep breath. Then her disposition changed. She clenched her jaw and crossed her arms. "I don't see why you're making us do so much of it for this class," she added in a combative tone. "It's not the subject. How much do I really need to know how to write anyway?"

"Listen, I know you've all heard me say this already," I explained. "Writing is an important skill. No matter what you do in life, writing well helps you. It pushes you to think clearly and to better communicate with others. Now, I know you guys can do it. You have to push yourselves. You have to try," I said.

The students probably thought this was the same old wrath. To my mind, however, my complaints were changing. They were becoming more urgent. Before, I'd just been upset when the students didn't do the work. But my anger had given way to fear and desperation.

"Before you leave, I want you all to know that I will call your parents," I said. "My goal isn't to get you in trouble. But I think maybe they can help you—and me—by seeing that you get to your homework."

"My parents don't speak very good English," said Pete. "You won't be able to talk to them. Unless you speak Spanish."

"Good luck getting my dad to respond," said Komal.

"Let me worry about that stuff," I replied. "Now please, I want you to have this paper done by Wednesday."

They all plodded out of the classroom. My stride was heavy, too, as I walked into the lounge. There were only about ten minutes left in the lunch break.

A few teachers were picking at the remnants of food on a glass plate centered on the lunching tables. I'd apparently missed out on some lemon squares. When it came to sweets, the Mount Pleasant teachers and I were in lockstep. Every week someone was in charge of bringing dessert for the group.

Wald was sweeping crumbs off the table when I sat down next to him.

"You look frustrated," he said.

"Some of my students flat-out refuse to do the homework," I said, opening a bag of corn chips. "We're a third of the way through the semester and some of them are already in dire straits."

"What are you going to do?" said Wald.

"What would you do?" I asked.

"Talk to them some more. Try to find ways for them to want to do the work," he said. "On the other hand, you can't force them to perform. If they fail, it's unfortunate. But they fail. Sometimes flunking opens their eyes."

Mount Pleasant's bell buzzed, and Wald and the others left to teach their sixth-period classes. I sat alone in the lounge.

Flunk? I thought to myself. That word is not in my vocabulary.

Flunking certainly had never been part of my school experience. I'd never endured real failure in my studies or at work. The thought of flunking students was agonizing, like imagining a battle with malaria. This semester could be the only teaching experience of my life. I couldn't let students flunk.

But maybe I wasn't being realistic. I certainly had enough perspective to understand Wald's impassiveness. Over the years, he had taught many hundreds of kids. The overcrowded and undermanned California public school system required that he spread his attention razor-thin. So some of his kids, unfortunately, flunked. Wald hoped that once he failed them, those students would never want to repeat the experience.

I had it a little easier than Wald. I had only the one class. But I wondered if he didn't have the more practical perspective. I walked over to Purcell's office, seeking a second opinion. He was on the phone, but waved me in.

"Hi, Steve. What can I do for you?" he said after hanging up. Purcell seemed a little more stooped than usual. I'd often wondered if he was sick. But every time I'd casually brought up his health, Purcell said that he felt fine.

"How's it going?" I said.

"Okay," he replied.

I launched into my dilemma, explaining what I'd just discussed with Wald. Purcell was a glass-half-full kind of guy, I thought. He'd probably tell me that the vast majority of my students would make it through the semester.

"What do you think?" I said.

The principal's body straightened, and his eyes opened wide, the way they had when I first pitched myself to him six months earlier.

"Steve, you have to try extraordinary things. Take extraordinary measures," he said. "None of these kids have to fail. You can get them through the semester. Your persistence and resources? Those are two of the reasons I brought you here."

Purcell's sudden pep, and his pep talk, startled me. Just like Wald had inferred, students fail classes at Mount Pleasant every year. Would an eyebrow be raised if one or two of my kids flunked? I doubted it. Was Purcell throwing down an impossible challenge? Occasionally I wondered if I was just a curious lab rat to him, an anomaly who sought out adversity and challenge. Purcell's demeanor undoubtedly brightened every time he got the opportunity to push me.

But then I stopped myself. Why wouldn't Purcell set a lofty goal for me? Why wouldn't the principal of Mount Pleasant High School want to see what's possible for each and every one of his students? He was doing his job—with passion—and my respect for Purcell went sky-high. Shouldn't the default expectation of each California public school be how all of its students can succeed, as opposed to how few can fail?

I left Purcell's office, and as I walked toward my car in the Mount Pleasant parking lot, I felt energized. Not one of my students, I thought, is a lost cause. If only my tiny mother were still alive to meet Doug Purcell: They were two high-octane crusaders for education, both wrapped in unexpected packages.

Pinpointing my students' biggest struggle was easy: the writing. They hated the writing. When I lectured and was able to channel the likes of Will Durst, or the day's subject matter was particularly juicy, the kids enjoyed listening to me. They often loved guest speakers. But when the follow-up to a lively presentation was a three-page paper, the students were tortured. Some of them, including Pete and Komal, struggled to write half the assigned amount.

I knew why the writing could be tough. Maybe the students were first-generation Americans, and English wasn't spoken in their homes. Or it was spoken poorly, or there wasn't one book to be found in their bedrooms. Their English classes might have been rough experiences. Or perhaps the kids figured that they'd ultimately be working in hair salons or machine shops and saw no need to learn anything so challenging that didn't have to do with the tools of such trades.

But I wanted to give them a different set of tools, which at least might allow them to consider other careers. One of my mission statements for the class was to teach the kids to formulate informed opinions. I felt like that ability could serve them very well, in politics, law, business . . . lots of professions. I knew decent writing would help to make them critical thinkers. I wouldn't rest until I saw some progress.

So I focused. Through teachers at Mount Pleasant and other connections in education, I hired a couple of part-time writing tutors. One Tuesday in mid-March, the kids walked into room 612 and were met by a total of three instructors. Once the students sat down, I introduced my lieutenants.

"I've arranged for some additional help. Martine and Sara," I said, gesturing toward the hired guns with my right hand, "will see that we get through some of the work that I hope to accomplish this semester. They'll make a special effort to see that everyone improves their writing."

Hiring additional help, as one might imagine, was unheard of at Mount Pleasant. The teachers and school district could never afford such a luxury. But I could, and I even imagined a day when California's decision makers would see the worth in, say, streamlining the state's bureaucratic education system so that writing tutors might actually be available for some of the state's students. After all, shouldn't public school funds be spent on the most impactful aspects of education?

Meanwhile my students met the added firepower—and expectations—with a collective groan.

"Mr. Poizner, does this mean even more papers?" said Tracy, resting her forehead in her hand. "I thought you'd let up on the writing after a while."

"How about giving us a break," said Pete.

I shook my head. I wanted the kids to like me and, despite all of my frustrations, I was growing to like many of them. Tracy was not only smart but funny—she'd give me grief about my seemingly endless supply of knit sweaters. Komal always had energy and something of substance to say. Pete regularly laughed and smiled. Even Jimmy had started raising his hand.

But that morning, I couldn't bear to hear the students' complaints about writing. The train, so to speak, had left the station. In fact, we were all on a metaphorical train, now rushing headlong toward a destination called Decent Prose.

I'd learned to focus—really, to *hyperfocus*—back in the days when I established SnapTrack. Ken Oshman, the venerable Silicon Valley entrepreneur who helped get my company going, once gave me some advice that I've heeded ever since.

"Focus on what you want done until it feels like you're too focused," Oshman had said. "When you have the courage to say no to many things? When you feel like you're leaving other opportunities on the table? Then you're almost focused enough."

I remember taking Oshman's advice for the first time when I turned down the military's request to somehow connect GPS technology to its special dolphins. I'd been reluctant to listen, even after the lecture where he told me I'd be insane to pursue such an obscure challenge. But I convinced myself to follow Oshman's words and to think big. Yes, SnapTrack desperately needed money at the time when the navy had made the inquiry. Still, I called the naval officers back and said no. And SnapTrack kept its focus on squeezing GPS technology into cell phones.

For the sake of improving the students' writing, I made cuts to my lesson plan. I reduced the days we spent on federalism, as well as on the media's role in government. I skipped a scheduled quiz. I'd hired help.

"We'll spend all of today and tomorrow working on improving your papers," I said to the class, the tutors standing beside me. Pete's shoulders sank.

"If I tell you to write a paper explaining the benefits of high voter turnout," I continued, "how would you approach the assignment?"

Nobody raised a hand.

"Okay," I continued. "What if I told you to give me six reasons why voter turnout in the U.S. is low? Where would you look?"

"In the voting chapter of the textbook," said Tracy.

"That's one place," I said.

"Go through my notes," said Joe.

"Good," I said.

"Look in the school library for books about politics," said Jimmy.

"Good stuff, Jimmy," I said. "That might take some extra effort. You'd have to dig for information about voting inside a general book about politics. But looking around for ideas is important. For example, you could ask a couple of people in your neighborhood if they vote. If they say no, ask them why not. And then you might have even more useful information."

"Can't we just make a list of points for you? Why write a bunch of sentences?" asked Komal.

"Because facts are only part of the story," I said to her. "You want to use those facts to create a thesis, which is an argument, or a big, central point that you're trying to make. You could decide to write a paper maintaining that higher voter turnout would lead to the election of officials who best represent the people. Then suddenly the talk you had with a neighbor about voting helps you make your argument. You could write something like, 'Because she works long hours and doesn't speak fluent English, she votes infrequently.'"

Komal nodded. "Yeah, if the polls were open later, and if ballots were available in different languages, then maybe voter turnout would improve," she said. "People would be happier with their elected officials."

"Is that idea about a thesis sort of what you did when you prepared the talk you gave to President Bush? The one about your mentoring program?" asked Joe.

"It's exactly what I did before speaking to the president," I said. "First I gathered a lot of information. Then I used it to help me make the argument that a large-scale mentoring program might benefit a lot of kids."

The students worked with me, and the tutors, on thesis statements. They also spent time on grammar and sentence-construction exercises.

For the kids, there was also some light at the end of the tunnel. We'd be doing something completely different in a couple of days. Sure enough, when Thursday morning of that week arrived, the class was standing in front of the school. The students watched as a giant Greyhound-style bus swung into the parking lot. We were embarking on our first field trip, to a youth rights conference at nearby San Jose State University.

The kids were excited to get out of the classroom. I was, too, and eager to see the upcoming three-page papers I'd assigned them about the dangers of student censorship. The topic would be addressed at the San Jose State event.

Organizing the field trip had been almost as big a battle as addressing the students' writing. The arrangements were a logistical nightmare. Purcell had to call the school district offices to get the okay for me to take the kids off campus. San Jose State was only about ten minutes away, but I had to arrange for the rental of a bus with a district-approved bus line. I also had to pay for the bus and the rest of the day's events. As usual, the school was way too thin on funds to support such a diversion.

I sat in the front row of seats, near the bus door. Much to my surprise, Jimmy sat down next to me.

"Ah, awesome view," he said, pointing to the bus's panoramic windshield while reclining in the seat.

Jimmy, like most of the kids, was in a great mood. The huge smile on his face showed off his straight, white teeth. I don't think I'd ever seen them before. You would've thought he'd boarded a plane for Hawaii instead of a bus for a brief drive.

"How many field trips have you taken since you started high school?" I asked.

"I think two," he said, tapping his fingers atop his thighs, as if electricity were running through his body. "You know Mount Pleasant. You can't get a water fountain fixed. Flat broke."

Unfortunately, the bus ride was just long enough for our conversation to nose-dive into an awkward silence. Jimmy and I had never been together outside the classroom. I'd only ever asked him questions about a lesson, or when he'd be turning in his late homework. He was currently pulling a D in American Government. He hadn't turned in every paper.

Nonetheless, the field trip's celebratory energy prompted a call for temporary détente. I took a deep breath and tried to forget about Jimmy's academic missteps.

"What are you up to this coming weekend?" I said to him.

"Hang with my buds," he said, shrugging his broad shoulders. "I'll definitely do some weight lifting."

"What about your family?" I said.

"My mom and dad work a lot," he said, rubbing his right forearm, the one with the twisted, ugly scar. "I might see them."

Jimmy caught me looking at his big scar.

"Got that when my friends and I ran into some unfriendly people in the neighborhood," he said, tracing the scar. "I won't be doing any of that nonsense when I'm in the marines. Gnarly, huh? Never had that cut stitched."

The bus came to a halt in front of the San Jose State campus, and our conversation ended. Just as well. I didn't know how I would have posed my next question—the one asking Jimmy if he was in a gang.

The kids and I all enjoyed the conference, and I took everyone bowling at the student union center after the event. I then looked forward to the papers on student censorship.

The following Tuesday, almost all of them turned in the assignment. That was an achievement in itself. When class ended, I went right to Jimmy's homework. He wrote:

I'd argue that we students deserve to be angry for being censored. Now I'm going to tell you the reasons why.

The Fourteenth Amendment says we should be treated farely by teachers and principles. If they want to suspend us they can't. Not without us getting to say "why," they can't.

Jimmy's thesis was basic. But it was a thesis. His paper was a bit longer than two pages, and he had included some good facts to back up his argument.

I remember Joe's paper being improved, too:

How would adults feel if they arrived at work every day and the first thing that their bosses said were, "We don't trust you." The adults would feel terrible and not want to be at there jobs. Students don't want to be at school either if they don't feel trusted.

Joe's grammar and spelling were off, but the paper was almost three pages long. It was full of decent arguments. I gave him a B+ and wrote "Nice stuff!" in big letters at the top of the first page.

A whole lot of focus, some positive results. I breathed a little easier.

There was another potential—and as of yet untapped—resource to help keep my students from the brink: their parents.

"I have to be honest with you, Steve. They can be harder to motivate than the kids," Purcell told me one March afternoon in his office. "Remember when you first came to Mount Pleasant, and I told you that this wasn't like an upscale Silicon Valley high school? That the kids weren't enormously motivated? The lack of motivation trickles down from somewhere, and sometimes it's the parents," he said. "I don't know how much magic you can work."

I'd already experienced some parent apathy. The memorandums of understanding—getting the last ones signed took considerable time. I didn't think reading and signing a document would take weeks.

I'd also sent a memo home with students months earlier about a potentially great opportunity called Close Up. The nonprofit foundation offers weeklong civic education programs in Washington, D.C., for middle and high school kids, and the programs include tours of the capital's iconic government buildings. Before the semester even began, Wald and Ellison had mentioned Close Up to me, and that every few years a modest group of Mount Pleasant students scraped together the necessary money to participate in the program.

I thought Close Up sounded so impressive that I offered partial scholarships to send approximately twenty Mount Pleasant students on the program during the school's April 2003 spring break. The memo had asked the parents if they were interested, and if they could help think of ways to raise a few hundred dollars for each kid. Scholarship applicants would also have to maintain decent grades, perform some community service, and write a paper to be eligible.

Wald and Ellison were appreciative and enthusiastic (I'd opened up the scholarship opportunities to their students and some others, too). But when it came to the kids in my class, the memo hadn't generated a response from more than a handful of families.

Close Up was only a month away; some of my students were receiving occasional Fs for their work, and even more were underachieving. It was time to see if some East San Jose adults could light a fire under their kids.

After talking to a dubious Purcell, I went home that evening and sat down at my desk. I had an alphabetical list of my students' names and phone numbers. One by one, I called the kids' homes.

"Hi, this is Steve Poizner. I teach twelfth-grade American Government at Mount Pleasant," I said into the message machine of Mrs. Lorita Boras, the mother of Antonio Boras. The phone machine's outgoing message had been in Spanish, which I don't speak.

"I'd like to discuss some strategies that might help Antonio do better in class," I said. "I think if we work together, we can improve his writing and get him to complete more of his reading assignments. I'd like to discuss an upcoming event, too."

I hung up and went to the next name on the list. I got another message machine. The message was in English. I stated my case again.

Next I called Mr. and Mrs. Gilberto Cardenas—Tracy's parents. Mrs. Cardenas picked up. I gave her my spiel.

"Tracy is a very bright girl, you should be proud of her," I added. "She's a good writer. Mrs. Cardenas, if we combined forces, Tracy could really nail her assignments."

"Thank you for your call," Mrs. Cardenas said in a gracious voice. "What can you do to make her work harder? I'd like for Tracy to succeed."

"I'm trying to make the most of our time in the classroom. But I think parents can help," I said. "Maybe you can see to it that she puts more effort into her homework."

"Tracy is in school all day so she can learn. Right, Mr. Poizner?" Mrs. Cardenas said, in a matter-of-fact tone. "I don't think she cuts classes. She tries to do her assignments. Are you calling because she's in some sort of trouble that I don't know about?"

"No, no, no," I said. "It's just . . . I think she can do better," I said. "She's sharp. I think she could be an attorney someday."

"Tracy has two younger sisters and a little brother, too. Her dad isn't around much. I'm really busy. I need to be at work every day at six in the morning," said Mrs. Cardenas. "As long as Tracy's not getting into trouble, I'm happy."

I asked Mrs. Cardenas if she'd seen the memo about Close Up, and she said no. She must've missed it.

I explained the program.

"We don't have the money or the time to think about raising extra money," she said.

"What about making a cake for a bake sale, or selling some old stuff at a flea market? Going to Washington, D.C., is a great opportunity for the kids," I added.

"No, thanks, Mr. Poizner," she said. "I have to go."

I called Pete Franco's house. A man answered, but couldn't speak much English. Was it Pete's dad?

"Encourage your son to do his homework," I told him, speaking slowly, as if talking deliberately were going to help me be understood.

I called another house: no answer. And another. On another call someone spoke to me in what I think was Tagalog.

The response from Joe Reardon's mom was effusive.

"Mr. Poizner, we can't thank you enough," she said. "Joe really appreciates what you're doing. He's really responded to your teaching."

Komal's dad couldn't be bothered.

"*Now* what's Komal up to?" Mr. Saldanha said before I could even finish my opening remarks. I could hear noise from a TV in the background.

"She's a great presence in class, Mr. Saldanha," I said. "She has a lot of energy and always has something insightful to say. But she struggles to get her thoughts onto paper. I'm worried about her completing enough work to pass the class."

"We may be moving before school ends anyway," he said abruptly. "This Close Up thing and your class. None of it may matter. But, you know. I'll see what I can do, Mr. Poizner."

Jimmy Vega's mom was subdued.

"We've tried with Jimmy. Honestly, it's been very tough with him. This is his second high school," she said, her voice sounding faint and ashamed. "He's gotten mixed up with the wrong people, Mr. Poizner. Sometimes we don't know what to do."

I hung up with Mrs. Vega and pushed my chair away from the desk. I looked at the picture of Nolan Ryan and his bloodied face. What would he do in the wake of so many sobering conversations?

The door to Rebecca's room was cracked open. I peeked in—she was happily playing on her bed with a pile of Legos. I thought about her private elementary school. The parents fall all over themselves at that place. Ask someone to bring in snacks, and the next day there's a bowl of perfectly scooped melon balls in front of every child. When one of the school's kids tests at only average levels, a flurry of solution-minded parent-headmaster meetings ensues.

I knew from my work in education that not every public school suffers from uninvolved parents. There are hundreds of California schools with fantastic parent associations, which generate all sorts of support and money. I applaud their efforts, of course—talk about embracing the entrepreneurial spirit.

Was it fair, I asked myself, to expect anywhere near as much out of Mount Pleasant's parents? I pictured Tracy Cardenas's mom getting up at the crack of dawn, and then coming home exhausted to deal with four kids. Maybe Mr. Franco wasn't able to take the time off from his job to learn English, and a lot of pertinent information wasn't reaching him. For all I knew, Komal Saldanha's dad had once suffered through a miserable education experience and expected nothing more for his daughter.

I told myself over and over that these parents and many of their peers likely already had their hands full. Many of them, I thought, were already giving parenting their all. They weren't *wrong* for placing a lot of the responsibility for their children's education on Mount Pleasant. They weren't to be faulted for not wanting to go above and beyond so that their children might earn Close Up scholarships. But I was unable to let go of the desire for wanting more for my students, even though I knew that changing the parents' lives in order to improve their kids' lives was an all but impossible job.

During the last week of March, Wald, Ellison, and I held a final meeting at the school for those interested in taking the Close Up trip to Washington, D.C. Maybe a dozen kids from other classes showed up—I recognized many of them from honors classes. But I couldn't convince a lot of my American Government students that the subsidized trip would be worth any amount of effort. Only a few of them attended.

I put a lot of faith in the man wearing the marijuana shirt. It was an early April morning, class was minutes away from starting, and in walked this bearded guy in his mid-fifties wearing a button-down shirt covered in a cannabis-leaf pattern. He was here, I reminded myself, to *prevent* students from flunking.

"Hi, I'm Dale Gieringer, from the National Organization for the Reform of Marijuana Laws," he said, offering me a relaxed handshake. Gieringer earned a Stanford PhD after studying the government's role in the regulation of drugs. He had happy, ruddy cheeks and a laid-back delivery. "Thanks for having me," he added.

Don't thank me, I thought to myself—not me alone, anyway. Before I started teaching my American Government class, I knew that I'd wanted my lesson plan to include a few in-class debates, complete with guest speakers who represented opposing perspectives. I thought that if the debates could touch on government-related issues and also be compelling, they could be successful teaching tools. Tension and healthy conflict, after all, were key ingredients in Hollywood blockbusters and bestselling novels. I thought those elements could work in the classroom, too.

Then I took the debate idea a step further: I empowered the students to choose the topics. I wanted them to feel like they had some say in their education, too. How many times at Strategic Mapping or SnapTrack had I come to the conclusion that *listening* had made me a much more successful boss? Krasner, my brainy SnapTrack engineer, was the guy with the huge technology ideas. I more often played the role of implementer. So when my kids voted for debates on the death penalty, racial profiling, and, to kick off the series, drug legalization, I consented. They were all issues, of course, that were relevant to the kids. My task was to make some calls and get the right talking heads to state their cases in our classroom.

But looking at Gieringer as he organized some papers, I was second-guessing my judgment. Personally, I'd not only never inhaled—I'd never felt the desire to take any drugs, and without question I oppose the legalization of marijuana. Yet there I was, standing next to Dr. Pot. Was he about to contribute to an inspired discussion that told the class something about the role and power of interest groups and public opinion? Or would the debate descend into an hour-long justification of why kids skip class to get high? Talk about providing my students with ways to avoid the midsemester blahs. Was I still a total amateur at this teaching thing, or what?

Even without hard evidence, I'd have been naïve to surmise that none of my kids drank or used drugs. (A 2005 study conducted in San Jose's East Side Union High School District would indicate that nearly one-third of its juniors had smoked marijuana, and more than half of them had consumed alcohol.) Plus Mount Pleasant's number of suspensions had nearly doubled between 2001 and 2002—and I figured that at least some of those suspensions were linked to illegal substances.

Too late to do anything now, I thought, and I introduced our guests to the class. Gieringer was California's coordinator for the National Organization for the Reform of Marijuana Laws, or NORML. I'd also invited two cops from the Alameda County Sherriff's Office to argue against the legalization of marijuana. One officer stood bolt upright and had an orderly mustache and a shaved head. The other was a broad-shouldered African American woman. Both wore suits.

"We'll hear Dr. Gieringer's argument for the legalization of marijuana, then we'll hear the officers' perspectives," I said with a half-smile. "Afterward we'll listen to rebuttals, and then open up the floor to questions."

Gieringer greeted the class and got down to business. "I often tell people that legalizing marijuana would benefit society. It wouldn't realize their worst fears," he said, stroking his beard. "Legalization could solve a lot more problems than it would create."

Gieringer said that legalizing pot could generate huge revenues for the state. He discussed how, in 1975, California's state legislature decriminalized the possession of small quantities of marijuana, and claimed that it saved the state many millions of dollars in prevented incarcerations. "It's been said that pot is less damaging to people than either alcohol or cigarettes," he added.

The kids listened intently, maybe more closely than I'd ever seen them listen. They nodded a lot, too. Where was this headed?

Gieringer went on a while longer, describing how California could fiscally benefit from a marijuana industry. "Like the wine business," he said. When he finished, the kids gave him a healthy round of applause.

Then the mustachioed cop stood up to speak.

"We'd argue that society doesn't want the burden of legalizing pot. It doesn't need the burden of legalizing pot," he said. The man talked in the terse style of a drill sergeant. "Legalizing marijuana would only increase crime. Add to the threat to public health."

The male officer then launched into a well-scripted monologue, exposing the sheriff's badge hooked to his belt every time he put his hands on his waist.

"Crime, violence, and drug use are frequently interconnected," he added. "The statistics don't lie. There are many more murders committed by those people who are on drugs than even those seeking out money to buy drugs."

The officer stopped short of his allotted ten minutes, ending by looking at Gieringer instead of at the kids.

"Your argument that marijuana is no more harmful to you than alcohol? Drunk driving is a big killer in America, Dr. Gieringer," said the policeman. "Do we want drugged driving so that we can add to the problem?"

Gieringer smiled a mellow smile.

"Please go ahead with your rebuttal," I said to Gieringer.

"Not every police officer continues in the futile attempt to enforce a law disobeyed by tens of millions of Americans," he said, slowly shaking his head at the cop with the mustache. "You're overstating the potential harm of recreational use."

"What defines recreational use of an illicit substance, Dr. Gieringer?" said the other cop, her arms crossed, her voice controlled but stern. "Did you know that drug use is down more than thirty-three percent in the last twenty years? We're winning the war on drugs!"

"Legalize pot and you'll eradicate a dangerous black-market industry!" said Gieringer, shrugging.

"Legalize pot and you'll increase usage!" she retorted. Her counterpart, meanwhile, was staring at Gieringer and turning red.

I looked at the kids' smiling faces. They were thoroughly enjoying the exchange.

"Thank you, officers and Dr. Gieringer," I finally interrupted, putting up my hands. "We're running out of time. I think the kids might have some questions."

I faced the students. Ever since they'd had nothing to ask FBI agent Michael Gimbel, I'd told the kids to prepare questions in advance. We'd gone over a bunch of them just yesterday.

"Tracy, I believe that you had a great question for the officers," I said, pointing to her.

"Do you have data proving that making possession a crime is the best deterrent for smoking pot?" she asked.

Officer Jones admitted that it was a solid question.

"Joe, I think you had a question to ask," I said.

"My question is for Dr. Gieringer," said Joe. "How would legalizing pot affect kids?"

Gieringer explained that, as with alcohol, great care would be taken to prevent kids from using marijuana.

"But alcohol is way easy to get," said Komal. "Do you think pot would be any harder to buy? Does NORML really speak on behalf of teenagers?"

That question wasn't in the script, I thought. But it was a good one.

"How would you convince older people, like parents, that legalized pot is okay. Like beer?" asked Jimmy.

I hadn't seen that one coming, either. From Jimmy, no less.

"Would we let cops decide if someone is too high? In making that determination, couldn't they be violating a citizen's rights under the Fourth Amendment?" Tracy asked.

Her insight blew me away. This was going great!

The kids wanted to continue even after the bell sounded. A good sign for the upcoming papers they'd have to write arguing who they thought won the day's debate and why.

"We'll continue this discussion tomorrow," I said in a triumphant tone. "Let's all give a round of applause to our visitors."

The kids clapped, and I patted the shoulders of Gieringer and one of the cops, as if I'd known all along that they were going to generate such a constructive conversation. As if I'd never doubted that maybe, given the students' own decision-making power and some subject matter that intrigued them, learning could be about as much fun as partying.

A few days later, Delaney walked by me in the social sciences lounge. I was seated, taking notes on some advice Wald was offering me about lectures leading up to another field trip. Set for mid-April, I was making arrangements to rent another bus for my class. I'd be taking students, class tutors, and Wald to visit San Francisco's U.S. Court of Appeals for the Ninth Circuit.

"What special arrangements are you making for your class now?" said Delaney, who seemingly never wanted me to forget that I was well connected and well off. He sat down at an empty seat across from me. "I thought you were trying to find out what it's like to be a *teacher*."

Watch out, I thought. Delaney is in a supremely nasty mood today. The other teachers in the room sensed his anger, too, and they quickly immersed themselves in whatever it was they were doing. Randall Nuñez lifted the newspaper he was reading in order to hide behind it. Sally Constell decided to rewash her salad fixings. Ian Ellison suddenly became very absorbed in some tests that needed grading.

"Pretty sweet, having tutors," Delaney added, chomping on a piece of cold pizza. "Everyone around here would like that. Idle time would be nice, too."

"Simon, where is this conversation going?" asked Wald.

"Oh, come on, Robert. Everyone knows you're Steve's little tool," said Delaney. "Can't he defend himself?"

I could.

"I think the kids are getting something out of me being here, Simon," I said in a very even tone. "I'm also learning a lot from them, and from you guys, too."

I wanted to say plenty more. How many times had Delaney paid a visit to my class, and watched me bust tail to keep the kids engaged? Zero. Was I really at fault for trying every little thing to help my students succeed?

But I didn't dare say more. I sensed that Delaney was understandably exasperated about the tough situation he faced daily: teaching 150 kids on a shoestring budget. As an outsider I also knew, after spending three months in the trenches at Mount Pleasant, that my relationship with virtually every teacher I came in contact with at the school was complicated. Tapping my many resources in the name of getting all my students through American Government only made the relationships more complex.

How could I argue too hard with Delaney when he was, to a degree, right? I didn't know what it was like to be a career teacher—year in and year out, preparing nine months' worth of lesson plans for several different subjects. I didn't know about trudging home exhausted after an eleven-hour day with a hundred papers in my arms, wondering how on earth I'd get them graded. I hadn't experienced the numbness that a teacher must feel when she knows that kids in her class will fail, and she's already too overextended to do much about it. If those tough rites of passage are required of teachers, then Delaney had me nailed: I was a poser.

At some level, I believe, all the teachers felt that way about me. Which is why those gathered at the social sciences lounge lunches always had at least one ear to the ground when Delaney unleashed on me. His peers weren't completely dismissive of Delaney's rants.

But I couldn't be called a poser without also being recognized as a sponge. I played the part of the social sciences department's wide-eyed rookie with utter sincerity. I took advice from anyone who would offer it to me. Ellison, Constell, Nuñez, Barbara Stevens, Dustin Martz—at one time or another, they had all given me guidance. I'd sought out Wald's advice repeatedly, whether I wanted lesson strategies or reassurances that I was grading tests fairly. One day when I was at wit's end over ways to motivate Pete Franco, I sent him to Wald. He gave Franco a hard-nosed lecture that I didn't quite know how to deliver. But after their talk, Franco turned in two late papers that I'd repeatedly asked him to finish. I was grateful.

Nonetheless, when it came to the Mount Pleasant staff, I could find myself in a social no-man's-land. Sometimes the teachers thought of me as one of their own. For instance, in the middle of the spring 2003 semester, I heard some faculty scuttlebutt that Delaney had once actively campaigned to keep me from ever landing my own class. I got the impression that the gossip made many of the other teachers wince.

"I think Simon believes in aliens," one Mount Pleasant staffer said to me in a sympathetic whisper. "He thinks there's something behind everything in life."

Meanwhile, my strong relationship with Purcell also distanced me from the teachers. The principal and I were both Republicans, although the friction between Purcell and the social sciences teachers had to do with far more than politics. A lot of the discord was a result of their professional roles. Being the school leader, Purcell rightfully agitated for change and constant improvement to better the students' education and applauded my efforts (and regularly sat in on my classes). Purcell was indeed "stirring up the system," as he'd once told me he'd hoped to do, by bringing aboard someone like me, who stopped at virtually nothing to get Mount Pleasant students working harder. On the other hand, the social sciences teachers were the school's overextended foot soldiers. They often had little choice but to think more about surviving than about reinventing. I appreciated both perspectives and yet felt caught in the middle.

"They're hard to handle, Steve. They're a difficult bunch," Purcell had told me before I'd begun teaching American Government, and he'd laughed a little when he'd said it. But to Purcell it was only a half-joke, and months later it dawned on me that his comment hadn't been about the students. Purcell was referring to a few teachers I'd regularly encounter in the social sciences lounge.

I made the best I could of the situation. I tried to stay focused on learning about teaching and public education and doing whatever it took to pass my students. Purcell didn't ask me for money and I didn't freely give it, although I happily bought the school a few PowerPoint projectors and made a contribution in support of a school magazine. I also donated about fifteen dollars for the Close Up trip to Washington, D.C.

Showing solidarity with the teachers, the students, and the administration, one sunny Saturday in April I attended a Close Up fundraiser. The event was a flea market held in one of Mount Pleasant's parking lots, and when the selling stopped, the area was a complete mess. People left behind all the stuff they couldn't unload, and then some: old clothes and shoes, ripped carpet padding, used diapers, leftover food—you name it. Wald, Ellison, and I oversaw the shuttling of heap after heap of unwanted belongings to the school's Dumpster-sized, rusty, and grungy trash compactor. At one point, garbage spilled out of the top of the machine. It was overfilled.

"What do we do now?" I asked Wald, who had stopped pressing the button that controlled the compactor. I kicked at a ratty shirt near my feet.

"Someone has to get up on the pile of trash in the compactor and jump up and down. Get it compressed so that the compactor can push it all into the bin."

I was wearing what I frequently wear: pressed khakis and rubber-soled loafers. Wald and Purcell displayed poker faces and said nothing. Finally I volunteered.

"Step from the platform onto the pile, Steve," Wald said, without a smile. "Be careful."

I probed with one foot until it felt supported atop an old carpet remnant. But when I put all my weight onto the pile, I sunk to my waist in a sea of paper plates, overfilled trash bags, and old clothes. The garbage smelled terrible.

"Good job, Steve," said Ellison with a huge grin. "Jump on out so we can fire up the compactor."

I considered Ellison and Wald two of my biggest allies at Mount Pleasant. But even they took more than a little satisfaction in watching the groomed and pressed multimillionaire sink deep into the school's trash.

CHAPTER 7

What Can I Do?

No doubt about it—I was delivering a boring lecture. But I wanted the kids to take in some basics about civil liberties, and I hadn't come up with ways to spice up every last fact. Little did I know that one mediocre class on a warm, drizzly Tuesday in late April would bring me to make a difficult admission: I didn't control my students.

"The Constitution includes two clauses about due process of law," I explained to the class, pacing up and down the center aisle of room 612. "Those two clauses address procedural and substantive due process."

The ho-hum topic left the air inside the room feeling heavy and thick. Between sentences, I could hear the buzz from the overhead fluorescent lights.

I spotted Pete picking at his pencil's eraser, and a girl two desks behind him quietly cracking her knuckles. I saw something else, too: a student playfully shoving his neighbor. The guilty party was Moe

Yuen, a bright kid and also a smart aleck and constant goof-off. He exasperated me like no one else in the class.

Moe delivered another friendly shove to the boy next to him.

I turned to look at the instigator. Moe frequently oozed attitude. His black hair was long and often hid his eyebrows, which arched mischievously. He had a wispy beard that came to a devilish point.

"Moe, please give me your attention," I said. He dutifully sat up in his seat.

"My bad, Mr. Poizner," Moe replied, with the sarcastic flick of an index finger.

"Procedural and substantive due process require that the ways government acts, and the laws it acts under, are fair," I continued.

I heard Moe chuckling behind my back. In a loud whisper, he then said something to someone about a Jay Leno monologue.

I turned around slowly.

"Come on now, Moe," I said, watching his darting eyes. "The sooner we get through these concepts, the faster we can get to some juicier material."

He gave me a gratuitous shrug and nod.

I resumed the lecture. "So how, you might ask, does the government define *fair*?"

Moe let out a laughing snort behind my back.

I wheeled around. "That's enough," I barked. "You're disrupting the entire class. This is the third time I've asked you to settle down."

"I won't do it again, Mr. Poizner," he said, trying unsuccessfully to suppress a smirk.

What Moe couldn't know in that moment—what I didn't know in that moment—was that his irksome smile brought me to a tipping point. I felt a rush of anger and did something I hadn't done once in my seven months at Mount Pleasant. I hadn't done it much in my professional career, or my life, either.

I went ballistic.

"That's right, you won't misbehave again, Moe," I said, clenching a fist. "You're done for today. Leave the classroom."

"Come on, Mr. Poizner. I'll pay attention," he said. But the grin on his face quickly gave way to doe-eyed concern. All the kids seemed surprised by my anger.

"Pack up your things and get out of this room right now!" I yelled.

"Mr. Poizner!" Moe said, flabbergasted. "I don't want to go. I'll behave." Tears rolled down his cheeks.

"Pack up your things, Moe!" I bellowed. "I hope you can bring a better attitude tomorrow."

Yuen tried to muffle his sobbing and gathered his belongings. I had already begun to regret my tirade.

When he walked out of the dead-silent classroom, the sound of the door latching behind him resonated. It felt like the air had been sucked out of room 612. The kids sat stunned, while I taught mechanically until the bell sounded. Then they all noiselessly filed out.

I stayed behind, alone in the classroom. I had little desire to enter the lounge and face a hostile Delaney or an unsentimental Wald. I felt horrible for yelling at Moe. I needed to sort out my feelings.

I'm not a yeller. I grew up in the library-quiet Poizner house. I didn't raise my voice much in school or as a businessman. When I first met Carol's family, I discovered that her siblings and parents were all huge sports fans. I was amazed at how they hollered during games, whether they were watching a fourth quarter unfold while in the stands or in the living room.

So what made me erupt? That my outburst had to do with personal defeat wasn't, at that very moment, apparent to me.

I did know that I had strong views about Moe. Thoughts unlike those I had about the other students.

Ironically, I wasn't worried about Moe faltering because of his work. He was capable, and his efforts were generally sufficient. Instead, I struggled with Moe's often dismissive attitude, which was shaped by forces that I imagined were pretty dark.

I'd never seen Moe before he appeared in my class about two weeks into the semester. He showed me his Mount Pleasant schedule and sure enough, my fifth-period American Government class was on it. Where had he come from? Moe took a seat, and after the period ended he told me that Purcell would explain his situation.

Later that same day, the principal informed me: Moe had recently been released from juvenile hall and was subsequently ordered to attend classes at Mount Pleasant. Purcell wasn't made privy to exactly what Moe had done to land in juvenile hall in the first place. Apparently such information blackouts in the handoff from detention center to public school weren't uncommon.

"You're lucky that boy arrived when he did," Wald later told me. "Sometimes we get paroled kids in the middle of the semester. Come out of juvenile hall and they have to go somewhere."

The middle of the semester? A teacher had to somehow instantaneously convert a kid's recently compromised past into classroom success? Especially when a supposedly troubled kid had to work double-time to catch up with his classmates? I thought that was ludicrous. Public school teachers aren't asked to be teachers. They're asked to be magicians.

In terms of pulling a rabbit out of a hat—that is, making sure Moe passed American Government—the two of us had gotten off on the right foot. I worked hard to bring Moe up to speed, and initially he was receptive to my efforts. But while his work improved, his conduct didn't. He talked over others, interrupted me, and indulged in distractions whenever he felt like it. Once, when Joe's dyslexia bubbled up while he read aloud to the class, Moe rolled his eyes. He called Joe "stupid."

I wanted to discuss Moe's behavioral issues with the adult supposedly responsible for the boy. But this person, who was characterized as a "guardian" on my list of class contacts, never returned my calls. I wasn't convinced that Moe had a guardian. Sometimes I wondered where he went at night.

Moe wouldn't volunteer information to me about his past, or any problems at home, either. When I asked Purcell if Moe could get help from a school counselor, he said that the few counselors Mount Pleasant employed already had full caseloads.

"I'm pretty sure the boy isn't a drug dealer," Purcell had said. "Work with him as best you can."

Yet Moe ultimately ran out of gas, and told me as much.

"That's enough," he'd once blurted out when we were having an after-class conversation a couple of months before I threw him out of the room. I'd been in the midst of offering Moe encouragement, telling him that he did good work and was capable of greater accomplishments.

But after hearing Yuen's harsh interruption, I unconsciously decided to comply. *That's enough,* I must've said to myself, because I began tolerating Moe more than teaching him, making an effort only so far as to keep him in check and producing decent work. Really, I'd taken Moe's rejection personally, more personally than the snubs I'd received many times as an entrepreneur. I didn't want to take his behavior so personally—but there was something very painful for me about trying to help a child and getting rejected in the process. So no, I didn't let Moe enter into the circle of American Government students that I grew to focus on, the circle that included kids like Joe, Tracy, Komal, and even Jimmy. Instead Moe sat on my emotional periphery. Thanks to Moe, I understood how teachers' hearts might harden.

Sitting alone in room 612 after my meltdown, I asked myself if Moe's bad behavior had been enough to fuel my intense outburst. Still a bit bewildered, I left just before sixth-period classes began. I went home.

Soon after arriving, I replayed the day's events for Carol. She was sitting at the desk in her office, sending e-mails. She had her back to me.

"I thought you took on this teaching project so that you could better understand California's crumbling school system," she said, spinning around in her chair to face me. "You know, because you're determined to fix the entire state," she added with a wry grin.

"Instead you seem very focused on prevailing in the classroom," she said. "As in, getting these kids to come around and do exactly what you want."

"Carol, the students' problems are emblematic of the entire public school system's problems," I said, slipping my hands into my pants pockets. "Moe Yuen is every kid in California who goes straight from a detention center to a classroom."

"I'm not trying to be unsympathetic. Undoubtedly, you shouldn't have yelled at that boy," she said. "But you've done a lot for him, and it sounds like he's doing all right in the class, at least academically. Isn't that enough for you? Exactly how far do you think you can take these children? Are you trying to . . ." She paused, and scratched her head. "Are you trying to *win*?" We looked each other in the eye for a few seconds. Then she shrugged, and spun back around to her desk.

Carol didn't know how right she was. I had come to Mount Pleasant to learn about California's broken education system, and I'd already absorbed a lot. She was correct in saying that Moe and many of his peers had made solid academic progress.

But what she made me realize was that I wanted much more than just exposure to a struggling public high school. I wanted something—a lot, actually—from Moe and the other students. Most of them had untapped potential, and there was a part of me that hoped I'd get the most out of each kid. Indeed, I had a semiwhimsical vision of a Hollywood ending to the semester. The over-the-top *Stand and Deliver*–type story, this time starring Steve Poizner and his utterly transformed students from East San Jose's problematic Mount Pleasant High School. After all, I'd made a habit of engineering so-called perfect endings. I'd been at the top of my school classes, invented a life-saving technology, made my own fortune, and so on. I'd achieved these successes because I'd demanded so much from myself. I was determined to shape many of my life's outcomes.

But as Mount Pleasant's spring semester entered its homestretch, the fact was sinking in that I wouldn't determine the outcomes of the thirty-plus seniors in my American Government class. I couldn't shape them like start-up companies, which are enormously unpredictable ventures of a different sort: enterprises packed with highly motivated Silicon Valley talent that, given the right ideas and timing, could be steered toward home-run-type sales or stunning IPOs. The kids weren't all going to become like me, bent on marching toward success. Instead, if some of my students didn't fail American Government, they'd probably limp across the finish line.

My Mount Pleasant class displayed a huge array of sensibilities and values. Plus, I had to remember, it consisted of *kids,* with their range of abilities, emotions, and histories, as well as screaming hormones, first driver's licenses, and early glimpses of adulthood. I was hardly the only force at work on their development.

Moe made me so mad because he was an in-my-face reminder

that, despite my resources and resolve, I couldn't transform him or the rest of the class. There was only so much I could do.

A night after coming undone in the classroom, I went to the movies with Carol. I sought a little levity, and I thought what better movie to put my frustrations into perspective than *Anger Management,* a comedy starring Adam Sandler and Jack Nicholson. Unfortunately, I don't remember much of the flick. While Carol enjoyed the show, I was again caught up in thoughts about my limitations in the classroom. I blamed my distraction on the smell of the movie popcorn. The vaguely chemical, buttery aroma reminded me of a high school job I once had, an old friend who was something like Moe Yuen, and a hotheaded boss.

I was about fifteen years old when I worked at Houston's Meyerland Cinema. The Meyerland was a two-theater movie house neighboring the Radio Shack where I'd browsed nonstop as a kid. My starting wage was a pittance, but nonetheless I initially had a good relationship with my overseer, Mr. Winchester. I did what the strict, perhaps twenty-five-year-old, assistant manager asked: took tickets, showed people to open seats, and threw out customers trying to sneak puffs on cigarettes. But once I became friends with Kevin Smith, Mr. Winchester liked me less and less.

Short, stocky, and blond, Kevin was different from me—a hangloose surfer type, with a rebellious streak that I'd be reminded of decades later in Moe Yuen. Kevin was smart and funny, too, and I was drawn to his humor and antics. Together we'd stuff ourselves with theater popcorn, or let our friends into the movies for free.

When *The Godfather* came to the Meyerland, Kevin and I established a defiant little tradition. As the movie approached the famous

horse-head scene, we'd blow off our responsibilities. Instead of working, we'd drift up to the front of the theater just seconds before the
guy who played Hollywood producer Jack Woltz wakes up in his bed
and pulls back bloodied sheets to uncover the head of his decapitated
horse. Kevin and I would face the audience as the drama unfolded,
and we never tired of seeing everyone's reaction. The disgust! The
shock! The pleasure two teenage boys got from watching a theater full
of people recoil in horror! I must have witnessed that moment dozens
of times.

Unlike me, Kevin constantly crossed Mr. Winchester. He regularly
ignored many of his superior's requests and loved to talk back. Mr.
Winchester thought he'd straighten out his problematic usher by
snapping at Kevin consistently. The harsh orders, however, never
resonated. Mr. Winchester was the one in a position to improve matters with his teenage employee. But he only made a bad relationship
worse.

One night, Kevin was part of the theater's closing crew. After
Mr. Winchester left, my friend changed the lettering on one of the
theater's marquees. The resulting message was X-rated and, to us
teenagers, hilarious. The Meyerland management, however, was not
amused.

Mr. Winchester ultimately decided to make an example of Kevin,
as well as of Kevin's good buddy Steve Poizner. We got the worst
chores in the theater. The boss was testing us: What kinds of employees were we going to be? Insubordinate ushers or perfect theater
soldiers?

Guess which path I chose, I remembered with a little shake of my
head, as Carol kept her eyes on the big screen while pawing at the air
beneath her seat. Her hand finally found the soda stowed on the
floor.

I took Mr. Winchester's harsh discipline very seriously. Too seriously. I cleaned the Meyerland Cinema's popcorn room—an entire room dedicated to an industrial-strength popper and copious amounts of cooking grease—as if it had never been cleaned before. Mr. Winchester then made me do it again. I scrubbed the bathrooms, too, and risked my neck by climbing a thirty-foot ladder to change lightbulbs in the sky-high ceiling.

Watching me in action, Mr. Winchester probably congratulated himself. But the truth was that he took advantage of a kid who always erred on the side of working hard. What if I'd fallen off that ladder and onto the unforgiving edges and angles of the theater seats below? Meanwhile, I don't think Kevin ever lifted a toilet brush before deciding he'd had enough of the place. In retrospect, Mr. Winchester could have handled a couple of high school boys a lot better.

I grabbed a fistful of Carol's popcorn and watched a few minutes of the movie. Adam Sandler and Jack Nicholson yelled at each other a lot.

Then I thought about my current standing at Mount Pleasant. Was I Moe Yuen's Mr. Winchester? Had I pushed him too much? Why did I give up on him? Why did I yell at him? Should I come down on him again? Were we destined to clash for the rest of the school year?

For months, I felt like I'd successfully kept the class in control. But my managerial gaffe brought other classroom dilemmas to mind. Why had I stopped making progress with a troublemaker like Moe, but inched forward with an apparent gangbanger like Jimmy? Why did Joe, dyslexia and all, agree to do extra reading, while I couldn't get Pete to get through ten pages of the textbook? What did other high school teachers have that I didn't, which helped them better understand their kids?

As the credits for *Anger Management* scrolled down the screen, I came up with an answer: experience.

I've had plenty of history as a manager, but with populations of professional adults. Teachers at Mount Pleasant, meanwhile, are accustomed to teaching kids from many different cultures, with different learning styles, who may or may not have a strong command of the English language. I could only imagine some of the nuanced moments of instruction, guidance, or encouragement that Delaney, Ellison, and Wald regularly provided. My peers certainly have had their Mount Pleasant success stories: students from their classes who went on to Ivy League schools, earned their way into Close Up programs, or been on award-winning debate teams. Plus Delaney, Ellison, and Wald had managed to pull the right levers in kids without the luxury of reaching into deep pockets.

The reality was that I didn't have their experience. Teaching veterans and education experts say it takes years of teaching to master classroom control, understand the psychological and developmental levels of individual students, and recognize how each kid will best learn. While Wald and Purcell in particular had been wonderful mentors to me, I still didn't have those years of experience to lean on. Instead there were six weeks left in the semester. I wouldn't be making many more gains in my teaching abilities. Really, I'd be finishing my classroom experience largely as I'd started it—feeling my way along.

The next morning, class began as usual in room 612. But the kids' odd silence and exemplary behavior during my forty-five-minute lecture only made me more aware, and ashamed, of my two-day-old outburst. Apparently it still had everyone on pins and needles. Even Moe listened attentively. I took no pride in the way I'd temporarily won everyone's attention.

After the bell sounded, a student named Donny Mates approached my desk regarding some homework. I wanted him to sit down and rewrite one of the three questions that I'd assigned each student to pose regarding the federal court system. His other two questions were fine.

Mates was another American Government underachiever. He was a strong student who, when he did the homework, contributed greatly to the class. But too often he was silent, presumably because he was unprepared.

As he pulled out his notebook and pen, I thought about how I'd pointed out Mates's academic missteps to him numerous times. I wondered if there would be much upside to me reciting all those shortcomings again. In the wake of my previous rant, I felt tentative. I took a different tack.

"Are you going to the senior prom?" I asked him.

Mates, a tall, good-looking African American kid with a big gold earring in his right ear, put down his pen and raised his left eyebrow. That wasn't a question he'd expected.

"Huh?" he said. "The prom?"

"Yes," I said. "Are you going?"

"No, not going to be there," he said, mustering a defeated grin.

"Why not?" I said.

"I don't have the funds, Mr. Poizner," said Mates. "I guess I'll find something else to do."

He picked up his pen and began to write.

Mates had some of Moe Yuen—and Kevin Smith—in him: attitude to go along with smarts. If only Mr. Winchester, Kevin's and my one-time, undoubtedly green manager, could've known how two of his Meyerland Cinema ushers turned out about forty years later: Kevin and I have remained close friends through the years, and he was the best man at my wedding. Kevin is also a fine electrical engineer and contributed greatly to my success at SnapTrack. Did he or I learn anything from Mr. Winchester? In spite of him?

I had an urge to pull a lever in Donny Mates. Would it hurt or help his high school experience if I added some sunshine to the kid's life? I took a little flier.

"Why don't we arrange it so that I pay for you and a date to go to the prom and to have some dinner beforehand?" I said after he showed me his work. "Let's figure out a way for you to go."

"You're joking with me, right?" he said. "You'd do that?" He broke into a sincere smile.

Then he narrowed his eyes. "What do you want in exchange?" he asked.

"Nothing," I replied. "Well, not exactly nothing. I mean, in a perfect world, I'd like you to apply yourself more in class. I'd appreciate you giving some guidance to the students who struggle. But I'm not paying you for those services. You're a senior. You should go to the prom."

"Man, I really appreciate that, Mr. Poizner," said Mates. He reached over my desk and gave me a firm handshake.

We discussed a few prom logistics, and then Mates left the classroom. It felt good to give him something from the gut instead of from a lesson plan. It also felt foreign.

"Let's hear the status reports on your community engagement projects," I said from behind the teacher's desk. "Why don't we go around the room?"

The spring weather had put everyone in high spirits. Outside it was sunny and warm, as it should be in early May. Jimmy wore one of his many tank tops, Pete was in shorts, and Komal was dressed in a flowery skirt.

But as the class wore on, I alone saw gloomy skies. I became concerned that, no matter what I did, the kids would fall far short on the semester's biggest assignment.

My students' grades would be heavily impacted by the execution of these community engagement projects. The projects, which were undertaken by students in groups of three and four, required that each team identify and focus on a problem in their community. Then the teams would have to address or perhaps solve these problems. Earlier in the semester, I'd suggested some project ideas: a neighborhood cleanup effort, a voter registration drive, or the creation of a group to reduce teenage drunk driving.

Picking out and taking on a problem represented only part of the assignment. The teams would have to present their findings, via PowerPoint presentations, at San Jose's City Hall in early June. Every team member would have to speak. I had arranged for Mayor Ron Gonzales and City Councilwoman Nora Campos to attend the meeting.

I was very happy with the idea. As with our in-class debates, I thought the community engagement projects added a wrinkle to the standard civics-class curriculum and pushed the kids to be on their toes and thinking in new ways. Plus, by clustering the students into small teams, I felt that the projects wouldn't place excessive pressure on any one kid.

The projects also touched on many of the elements that I'd incorporated into my semester-long lesson plan. The subject matter related to government or policy making; the research demanded that students get the pulse of a larger community; and the presentation required that the kids form written opinions, which they'd then use as PowerPoint scripts at City Hall. Landing the mayor was icing on the cake. I was excited for the students to know that city leaders would listen to what they had to say.

Purcell loved the concept, and signed off on it long ago. The students had picked their topics weeks earlier. But after receiving a couple of status reports, I worried that the kids and I weren't seeing eye to eye on execution.

"We decided that setting up at Eastridge Mall would take us too much time, so we didn't go there," said Pete to the class. His team had launched a voter registration drive, with the hope of signing up seventy-five new voters. "We only got permission to set up on the school's senior quad as of June first," he added, "which would be too late."

He nodded to his two partners and then looked at me.

"All right, Pete," I said. "I appreciate the update. Where will you go from here?"

"We'll start preparing the PowerPoint presentation for next month's meeting with the mayor," he said in a relaxed tone.

"Okay," I said in a calm voice. "Sounds like you've run into some difficulties getting out. Have you registered a fair number of people?"

"We've tried, Mr. Poizner," Pete said. "We've each already spent several hours on the project, and we haven't yet created the Power-Point presentation, which will take up more time."

I folded my hands together and took a long breath. I didn't like where this exchange was headed.

"How many voters have you registered?" I asked.

"I think we've registered twenty-seven," he said.

"And do I recall correctly that we agreed on a goal of seventy-five?" I asked.

Pete said yes. I waited for him to somehow acknowledge or apologize for the project falling so far short of the goal. But there was no such admission. Pete only looked at the fingernails on his right hand, seeming completely at ease. The room fell silent.

"Will you attempt to register more?" I finally asked.

"We'll see how long it takes to make the PowerPoint presentation first, Mr. Poizner," he said. "If we have time, maybe we'll try again."

Pete's team had attempted a food drive before launching the voter drive. Six weeks ago, he'd informed me that he'd contacted numerous stores without receiving any donations. When I told him that his group should try a different community engagement project that would generate results, he was dismayed at the idea of having to start over.

I guessed that his voter drive represented a second effort, which counted for something. I decided to move on.

"Okay, Pete," I said. "Please consider signing up more people. It's a great way to help the community."

I turned to Jimmy. "How did things go over at the elementary school?"

Jimmy cleared his throat.

"Well, we told some kids and their teachers that child safety, you know, maybe installing car seats, or watching out for lead poisoning if you tear down part of your house, is important," he said with hesitation. I could count on one hand the number of times Jimmy had really taken the floor this semester. His nasally voice was shaky and barely audible.

"And little children shouldn't be left alone with a dog, in case they pull their tail or annoy them," he said. "The dog might bite."

"All good information, Jimmy," I said. "Were you able to investigate where people can get help properly installing their car seats? Any statistics yet on the number of car seats that aren't installed correctly?"

"No, we didn't get that information," he said. "I mean, not yet."

"Uh-huh," I said. "I see."

I actually found our exchange encouraging. Jimmy had never before admitted that an assignment might benefit from more work. And this was the first time I could recall him ever appearing vulnerable.

I didn't feel comfortable asking him for more, especially in front of the whole class. Such a request could wait.

"Thank you, Jimmy," I said. "I'll check in with you later. Please keep up the good work."

I turned to Komal and nodded.

"Okay, we've talked to sixty-two people on campus," she said in a loud and confident voice. "We asked them seven questions each. We asked them whether or not CD players should be legal on campus, and if Mount Pleasant's tardy policy is fair, and if the no-hat rule should be changed. Things like that."

"Good stuff, Komal," I said. "How many people did you set out to talk to?"

"Forty-five," she said with a smile. "We're ready to move on to the PowerPoint part."

The rest of the class time was spent hearing updates on the other projects. They addressed air pollution and health insurance coverage, racial profiling and driving under the influence. Many of the kids' status reports revealed data that, unlike Komal's, was woefully thin. I decided to take it up with Purcell instead of dressing down any one group during class.

"I can't go out and do the research for them, Doug," I said in Purcell's office that spring afternoon. "Lots of the projects won't come close to their stated goals. How about a voter drive that's been in the works for a month and a half and has only twenty-seven signatures?"

Purcell was dressed in a tie, which he often wore. For better or for worse, dressing up separated him from the rest of the faculty.

"This is one time where I'd caution you not to push too much," he said. "The students are making calls, talking to people, and addressing issues that usually don't concern them. Don't forget, they're teenagers. They're preoccupied with their haircuts and coming up with gas money. The projects are demanding. I think they're as much about process as about outcome."

I leaned back in my chair, which was facing Purcell's desk. I watched some students walk by his office windows. I saw Tracy Cardenas talking to a friend and laughing. Was I wrong to wonder why she wasn't working on her community engagement project? Wasn't this a good opportunity to poll kids on their thoughts about abortion?

"I hear you. I'll heed your advice. But it won't be easy," I finally said to Purcell. "I can't help but want more."

"You're doing plenty," he assured me. "You've got the students out of their comfort zone."

Purcell was right about that. I was out of my comfort zone, too, and for the umpteenth time during my tenure at Mount Pleasant.

I no longer entertained some of the once-lofty visions I had for these projects. When I conceived of the idea for community engagement projects before the semester began, I envisioned my students creating a teenage drinking prevention program in conjunction with the Santa Clara County district attorney's office. Or a team of my kids joining forces with San Jose's Environmental Services Department to clean up some grungy East San Jose neighborhood. Instead, I anticipated presenting the mayor with a voter drive that garnered fewer than thirty signatures. How long would the meeting run before he looked at his watch? What kind of impression would Mount Pleasant leave on San Jose's city leaders?

I couldn't do much more than wait and see.

I'm sure no one enjoys that feeling of helplessness. I've had moments—too many, in fact—where losing control has unhinged me. Instances where my smarts, a strategic plan, or a veteran school principal couldn't improve the circumstances. But then again, it's hard to summon much strength when you face losing what's most important to you.

Almost two years to the day before the students updated me on their community service projects, in the spring of 2001, I received a late-night call from my mother. She said that my eighty-six-year-old father had died.

My dad's decline, of a rare degenerative brain disease called progressive supranuclear palsy, had been miserable. My parents moved into a San Diego retirement community in the late 1980s, and my father subsequently began suffering from the disease's effects. His vision was compromised and his movements took on a stiff, Tin Man quality.

My dad was quiet, but he had a lot of dignity. Unfortunately, the PSP took away his pride, too. He slurred his words, and struggled to swallow. When I'd visit my parents, I tried to remember the entrepreneurial Houston geologist walled inside of my dad's hardening body. But there were days when it was all I could do not to close my eyes as my aging mother attended to my failing father's multiplying needs.

PSP, however, didn't just lead to one death. It caused two.

I flew to San Diego the morning after my mother had called me with the news about my dad. I knocked on her apartment door, and nobody answered. I knocked again and called out to her, too. Still no response.

I didn't have a key, and when I found an attendant he swore that he'd seen my mother earlier that morning. I got anxious. Where was my mom? She knew I was coming.

Minutes felt like hours before a staffer finally slid a key into the lock of my mother's apartment door. When it swung open, my worst fears were realized.

Like I said, I'm not sure anyone enjoys feeling powerless. I sure don't. To find my eighty-seven-year-old mother on the apartment floor, felled by a massive stroke, and dying within twenty-four hours of my father's passing, was almost impossible for me to grasp. This couldn't be happening. Both of them gone?

In a single day I went from having a mom and a dad to being orphaned. You can be fifteen years old or coming up on fifty when you lose your parents, and the profoundly sad feeling is the same: you're alone.

And I was angry that my father suffered so much at the hands of a disease that modern medicine couldn't figure out, and depressed that PSP completely wore out my mom, who refused to leave my deteriorating father's side.

"You can be anything you want, Stephen." The words my mother spoke to me as a kid rang in my head. But I couldn't elevate myself into some higher power capable of bringing back my mother and father. Burying them at the same time was one of the hardest moments of my life.

Four years after the abrupt death of my mother, Carol assured me that I wasn't about to face a comparable tragedy. It was brave talk coming from a woman headed into the operating room for open-heart surgery.

Carol's pulmonary valve was failing. This didn't come as a complete surprise, because Carol was born with a hole in her heart. She'd been in the hospital twenty-two times by the time she was five years old. She was still a little girl when she had surgery to repair the hole, and the procedure had compromised her pulmonary valve. Forty years later, the valve needed replacing.

When she gave me the bad news, I reminded myself of Carol's resilience. As a baby, the doctors thought they'd lost her a number of times to pneumonia. Yet she'd always pulled through. She'd endured a lifetime of severe asthma. In January 2000, on the same day I closed the billion-dollar sale of SnapTrack, Carol called me in tears to tell me that she had breast cancer. But when she caught her breath, she promised me that we'd beat it. She bravely endured months of radiation and chemotherapy, and to this day she's cancer-free.

I knew Carol was tougher than me. I'll do anything to avoid getting shots or having blood taken. Needles bother me. When Carol was pregnant with Rebecca, and I watched the amniocentesis, the supersized needle wielded by the doctor made me woozy. My wife had to get up so that I could lie down.

Before Carol had the open-heart surgery, I found the nation's best doctors. Luckily, they were at Stanford—virtually in our backyard. I understood that the procedure required Carol to be put on a heart-lung machine to keep her blood circulating while the doctors "unhooked" her heart to replace the pulmonary valve. The bypass procedure, I was told, took about five hours in all. When I kissed Carol before she was anesthetized, I told her and myself that everything would be okay. Carol told me that, too. But I feared that I might never see her alive again.

Three hours later, Carol's surgeon entered the waiting room. What was he doing here? The surgery was supposedly far from over. My in-laws watched me turn as white as a sheet.

The procedure, the doctor told me, went phenomenally well. Carol would be fine. Later I walked into her room inside the intensive care unit, and despite all the tubes running out of her, Carol was awake and wanted to tell me something. She couldn't talk, so I handed her a pad and pen.

"Turn on *Survivor*," she wrote, thrusting her chin toward the TV. She wasn't kidding. The show was about to air. I could only grin. That woman has strength that I can't touch.

But not every Poizner who suffered a huge medical setback was able to get back on his feet. Jake, my family's sweet and affectionate golden retriever, did all that he could to rebound from adversity and land on four paws. Not long after Carol's operation, I entered into a yearlong odyssey to save Jake from cancer. When I told a friend of mine that I was prepared to do anything for the dog, he didn't mince words. An eyebrow raised, he told me that I was crossing the line from pet lover to dog fanatic.

"Aren't you going overboard, Steve? There are lots of worthy causes out there that could use your time and money," he said.

I was unrepentant. I was already deep into the work of helping California and its public schools.

"I'm doing what I can to give back to the world," I responded. "I think I'll indulge myself to try to save a member of my family."

Growing up, my mom and dad didn't let us have them, but now all of the Poizner children have dogs. Dogs are eternal optimists, and simple. They live to be happy. Plus for years my golden retrievers have gotten me out of the house to take half-hour walks in the neighborhood hills. They function as cheap personal trainers.

Unfortunately, I ended up taking care of Jake more than he took care of me. He was a good boy—sweet and calm—and he loved to have his belly rubbed. When he was a puppy he'd get very excited by his toys, once swallowing a chewy critter whole. Removing it required stomach surgery. We still have the X-ray showing the dinosaur toy in his gut. In the image, it looks like Jake ate a mini T. rex.

My semester of teaching at Mount Pleasant was still fresh in my mind when Jake fced another medical issue. This time he was diagnosed with stomach cancer.

Jake and I flew Southwest Airlines to Colorado, to visit some of the country's best veterinarians. They had the equipment to give Jake MRIs.

The doctors ultimately discovered that the cancer was wrapped around his organs and inoperable. Back home, Jake received chemotherapy and radiation. The treatments trashed his kidneys, but I wasn't ready to give up. I don't think he was, either. Not when, every once in a while, Jake would eat some food out of my hand, wag his tail, or seem like his old self, albeit on a walk that might extend only to the end of our short driveway. We both treasured each step.

Every day for six months, Jake gamely received an intravenous solution from a veterinarian's assistant who came to our house. When my dog finally took his last short breaths, I knew I'd taken every possible step to be with a creature that I loved. To this day, Jake's ashes sit in a box, next to one of his old chew toys, in our master bedroom.

Believe it or not, time also felt precious when I taught at Mount Pleasant. Particularly when the spring 2003 semester began winding down. I wanted to do what I could to avoid losing the heartbeat of anyone in room 612.

"Komal," I said as fifth period came to a close one day in mid-May. "Please come talk to me after class."

A couple of minutes later, the bell sounded. Komal, her ponytail bouncing behind her, approached the desk. Everyone else left the room.

In my mind, I tried to sort out exactly how I'd address my concern. Komal's work remained schizophrenic. I wanted her to bring her writing up to the level of her class participation.

"Hi, Mr. Poizner," she said, twirling a pen in her hand. Komal never seemed low on energy. "What do you want to talk about?"

"First off, I want to compliment you, Komal. Your contributions during last week's death penalty debate were fantastic. They were informed and well articulated," I said. "It's obvious that you do the reading and you're a very careful listener. I'm excited about all the work you've done with your community engagement project, too. You're a joy to have in class."

I paused. Komal's rosy cheeks lifted. "Thanks a lot, Mr. Poizner," she said. "You've made the subject kinda cool."

"In these last few weeks," I added, "I'm hopeful that we can bring your writing closer to the level of your other work."

Komal's smile disappeared at about the speed of light.

"Before you get frustrated," I said, holding up a hand, "I think we can easily address some of these issues."

Then I flipped through a pile of graded papers on the death penalty, which were stacked on the left side of my desk. I found Komal's work and pulled it out. I set it between us, faceup.

I'd written on the paper's front page, at the top, in red ink: "Please revise. Hoping for a more polished draft." I'd marked the paper with a D.

"That can change," I said, pointing to the lousy grade.

"You know the pros and cons of the death penalty, Komal," I said. "I heard you recite them in class. Maybe when you're home and trying to write these papers, you can say the points you'd like to make out loud. That might help you write a clearer thesis statement. Once you do that, your arguments will be easier to make. What you handed in feels unfinished."

Komal crossed her arms.

"I told you before that I hate writing and I'm bad at it," she said. "Why do you keep pushing me on this? I do a good job otherwise. You said so yourself."

"I've explained that I value good writing skills, Komal. I know you can do it," I responded. "I'm sure of it."

"My dad already thinks I spend too much time on your homework, Mr. Poizner," she said, her voice trembling. "He says things to me like, 'Why are you wasting your time asking a bunch of kids if they think CD players should be allowed on campus? Who cares?' And he's still threatening to move us, even before graduation."

Komal paused, apparently to gather herself. "You say I need to do more," she said in a steadied voice. "I don't like doing *some* writing, and you're making me do *a lot* of it. And my dad is coming down on me, Mr. Poizner. It's all a total drag."

I listened closely, and was grateful that Komal hadn't cried. One student and all the anxiety his tears had brought me was enough, I thought.

Her emotions did serve as a reminder. I was working in a high school, not a Fortune 500 company, or a hard-nosed start-up. As Purcell had said, I was teaching kids—adolescents preoccupied with their hair and allowances. Did I need to practice more empathy and patience? Those are important qualities in a leader, too, and I always tried my best to treat my companies' employees fairly. Plus, I had some clue of what it feels like to endure personal struggles. I've gone through the awful deaths of my parents, and Carol's scary near misses.

But I couldn't let up on Komal. Not on the writing. Her writing remained subpar, and she had to work to the same standards that I'd set for her classmates. Her situation at home might very well have been dreadful, but that couldn't totally cloud my judgment. The number of times Pete alone had blamed his lack of schoolwork on family troubles were enough to desensitize me.

"Why don't we compromise, Komal," I said. "You don't have to redo this paper. I know you know the material. But I expect to see a lot more effort in your final writing assignments."

"I don't want to try harder," she said, her arms still crossed. "Aren't I already doing enough work to pass? Isn't what I'm doing enough to get by?"

Her argument caught me by surprise.

"I'm sorry?" I asked. "What?"

"If I can just pass the class, I'll get my diploma," she said. "That's more than my dad ever did."

I had no ready comeback. In fact, Komal's lack of enthusiasm for trying harder made me—even momentarily—wish that I were in a different education universe. For months, I'd volunteered time outside of Mount Pleasant to bolster the California charter school movement. I'd worked with its leaders and leading benefactors, and had just put the finishing touches on the draft of a strategic plan that could serve as a solid road map for charter school expansion in the state. I like that charter schools are public schools, *and* that they operate with considerable independence. Another reason I was so interested? The schools often make great effort to customize curriculums and champion the benefits of attending college, so that students are more enthusiastic about doing their best instead of just trying to get by. I thought maybe charter schools could ultimately have a positive influence on traditional public schools.

But Mount Pleasant and its students still played by the conventional rules. There was no simple way for me to convince Komal of the upsides to working harder. Obviously I hadn't yet pulled the right lever inside her.

"Technically, you're right. You're doing enough to pass," I said. "I don't know your plans, but if you're considering going to college next fall, or if you ever want to go to college, you'll want to get good grades now. You know, good grades reflect what you've learned. There's no crime in learning a lot."

"I don't know my plans, Mr. Poizner," she said.

"Think about what I've said," I replied. "I still expect to see better writing from you."

Komal looked around me, instead of into my eyes. Then she stood up to leave.

CHAPTER 8

They All Deserve Better

"Glad I'm not you," Wald said to me as he looked at a thick pile of my kids' homework. It was the third week of May. I was sitting at the clustered lunch tables in the teachers' lounge and was in the middle of making an initial run through the students' last papers of the semester. Wald sat to my left.

"It's a lot of work, no doubt," I said, grabbing a brownie off a plate centered among the tables. The dessert came courtesy of Sally Constell—it was her turn to bring sweets. The sugar spikes added to everyone's already high spirits: Summer was on the horizon.

I was happy for other reasons, too. Mount Pleasant's school year had been a long haul. The more I'd taught, the more I understood how tough the profession was. My volunteer work in the California charter school movement had only deepened that appreciation. Yes, I thought to myself: I was glad I wasn't Wald.

I glanced at a couple of papers.

"Hey, I'm proud of these kids," I said. "You know Komal Saldanha?"

Wald shook his head.

"You know, ponytail, wears a lot of hooded sweatshirts, bounces on her feet, endless energy?"

"Oh, yeah," Wald said.

I held up her paper on civil rights.

"Best effort of the year," I said. "Not great, but better. I'm just happy she tried."

Wald glanced at all the comments I'd made on Saldanha's first page. "You get credit, Steve. A lot of teachers love teaching," he said, shaking his head. "Not so many teachers love grading papers."

Simon Delaney, who was sitting to my right, craned his neck to get a glimpse of the paper.

"That's a lot of work. Are you doing it for the students?" he asked abruptly, with cool disdain. And to think that Delaney and I had just been having a fine conversation about his honors students who were bound for San Jose State. I wondered exactly where his comments were headed.

"Or maybe you're doing it to prove that teaching can be done differently? Or should be done differently?" he continued. "Maybe it's all about conservatives wanting to find fault with traditional public schools. You know, so that you folks can call for a bunch of change."

I would rather have kept looking at the students' papers than engage with Delaney. Honestly, I would've liked a moment to kick back in my rickety chair with more chocolate. The brownies were excellent.

I sank my teeth into Delaney's bait instead.

"Simon, I'm very aware that I teach a fraction of the number of kids that you do. I don't pretend to think that it'd be practical for you to assign the writing work that I've assigned. Or that it's even the right thing to do. It's what I chose to do," I said.

"As for calling for a bunch of change, as you say," I continued, "maybe you're referring to my volunteer work with charter schools. But I'd argue that all the efforts I'm making nowadays with charter schools are also in the name of improving traditional public schools like Mount Pleasant. I want all public schools to get better."

"Rich men like to privatize things," he said, with a dismissive wave of his hand.

"That's not what this is about," I insisted. "I've been trying to get my arms around public education for months. I've been giving it my all here, figuring out how everything works."

I can't remember what Delaney said next. I know he didn't let up. Fortunately our clash didn't lead me to having a meltdown like the one fueled by Moe Yuen. I kept my cool.

I do recall not saying what I wanted to say to Delaney. It would've only poured gasoline on an already heated exchange. I wanted to tell Simon Delaney that he deserved better.

Not just Delaney. Robert Wald, Ian Ellison, and Sally Constell deserved better. The other teachers in the lounge? They all deserved better, too. So, for that matter, did their students, and their students' parents.

Of course, I didn't dare say any of that. I would've sounded like a condescending jerk. But my snowballing work with the charter school movement—I was in the middle of helping to shape a high-powered, statewide charter school umbrella organization—had given me some perspective.

Charter schools were different from traditional schools like Mount Pleasant in ways that I thought were sometimes superior. I believed that the possibility existed for California's charter school movement to grow, and ultimately to have a positive effect on the state's entire public school system. I saw a day when teachers and students throughout the maligned public school system could thrive. Despite Delaney's convictions, I didn't want to arrive at that happy point by privatizing all of public education, or plowing under Mount Pleasant.

I hadn't even known all the ins and outs of charter schools before coming to Mount Pleasant. Rebecca had long attended a private school, and I'd been swimming in a start-up fishbowl for twenty years. An education-reform-related article that I'd read in *The Wall Street Journal*—a compelling story about the California charter school movement that had appeared before I quit Qualcomm in 2001—helped introduce me to the concept.

Reed Hastings was also an invaluable guide. Hastings is a successful entrepreneur (he's currently the CEO of Netflix), and just about the time we met he'd begun serving as president of California's State Board of Education. Hastings was mentioned in the *Journal* article, and after reading the story I contacted him. Hastings was not only passionate about education, he was a big proponent of charter schools. He confirmed for me that charter schools receive monies from the same federal, state, and local funds as traditional public schools.

He also explained that they're called charter schools because they've been given a "charter," or license to operate, by a district, county, or the state. They can be created and organized by groups of teachers, parents, or a community-based organization. California has more charter schools than any other state in the nation.

Charter schools immediately appealed to me because they sounded like public education's version of a start-up business: If a charter school's ideas, management, and execution were solid, it had a chance to thrive. After all, SnapTrack became a success only because Norm

Krasner, some other key employees, and I managed to create a solid company around the idea that putting global positioning technology into a cell phone was a smart way to find people in emergency situations. In other words, we built a better mousetrap. The beauty of charter schools is that any civic-minded, highly motivated group of people can build a better educational mousetrap. And like a start-up company, a charter school suffers little at the hands of bureaucracy or inertia.

Thanks to Hastings, I made some initial forays into the charter school movement before arriving at Mount Pleasant. I made donations to investment funds and advocacy groups that championed charter schools and other aspects of education reform. I landed spots on a couple of education-reform-related boards of directors.

I also learned that opening, sustaining, or succeeding with a charter school isn't easy. Silicon Valley features a lot more tombstones than billionaires—many an entrepreneur has failed. Charter schools have failed too, often because of poor leadership or execution. Such setbacks aren't just a letdown for the charter school movement. A teacher caught in a compromised environment who is unable to perform at his best for even one student is aware of the loss for that student, and ultimately for society.

But the longer I taught at Mount Pleasant, the more I wondered if *any* of its teachers felt that they were in a position to deliver great educations. Mount Pleasant teachers had very limited resources, few opportunities to follow their professional instincts, and the support of only a handful of school counselors. How many student-discipline issues took teachers away from teaching? How many times did I hear teachers complain that their California-mandated programs were out of step with the needs of their students and classrooms? That their U.S. history class wasn't relevant to the kid who'd just arrived from

Vietnam? That their brightest students became bored when the class had to slow down for students struggling with their English?

My peers at Mount Pleasant often encouraged me to go look for all the wasted public school resources inside the state's centralized education bureaucracy. They ultimately called my attention to the fact that more than half of California's hundreds of thousands of primary- and secondary-school public education employees work outside the classrooms.

"What are all of those people doing?" Wald would ask.

He was right. What were they doing that was more important than what Wald and his peers were doing in the classroom with students? Why not, in fact, let Wald and his fellow teachers actually do some of the things that the bureaucrats supposedly do, like help design California public schools' curriculums and tests? It seems to me that teachers are in the ultimate position to know what works and what doesn't for the state's students.

Meanwhile, every time a news story appears about the meager performance of California's students, the teachers take it on the collective chin. Politicians and parents are quick to accuse instructors of failing, when so many other factors play a part in the education dynamic. But it's harder to place the blame on faceless institutions like resource-poor schools and bloated central government offices. Perhaps staffers in those HQ cubicles should be held accountable for student performance, too.

In spite of all these knocks against California's traditional education system, I seldom attempted to push my opinions about charter schools in the social sciences lounge. To public school teachers, the charter school movement can feel like just one more threat to their livelihoods. Money used to support a charter school often means there's less money available for existing schools. Plus a rising tide of charters could ultimately threaten teacher tenure, and force public school teachers to rethink their teaching methods. When I added up the perceived negatives, I felt that some of Mount Pleasant's teachers were more comfortable with the devil they knew than with the charter school they didn't.

I wasn't convinced that charter schools were the metaphorical white knight that could unquestionably save California's public education system. California has a lot of very good traditional public schools. But it also has many that struggle, and charter schools represent an infusion of energy, an X-factor that over time might work well enough to shake up an entrenched and ineffective bureaucracy. Maybe, I thought, there'd be a day when Robert Wald would feel energized instead of drained at the thought of grading a pile of kids' papers.

Wald, as well as Ellison, Delaney, and the others, were all hardworking people trying their best at extremely challenging jobs. But from where I sat, the traditional public education system seemed to be sapping them of their vitality. The fatigue was even reflected in the dreary social sciences lounge. Besides the broken copier and the wastebaskets that doubled as rain catchers, the lounge's walls were covered with yellowing news headlines, dusty books, and snapshots curling with age. The lifeblood had been drained from the lounge's décor.

The lounge's walls, by the way, also hosted half a dozen old images of Mount Pleasant kids participating in extracurricular activities. One of the photos was of the "mock trial team" and had rows of students, many of them in ties and formal skirts, all with medals draped around their necks. The caption read, "Mt. Pleasant High School Santa Clara County Semifinalists."

But by the time I'd arrived at Mount Pleasant, the school didn't have the money for all of its past programs. The teachers often mourned the end of those days, and I was even asked to hit up Purcell for funds to restart such activities. As if the principal had a secret stash of discretionary money and was waiting for me to make my requests.

On that oddly upbeat and yet tense May afternoon in the social sciences lounge, the brownies were long gone and the topic of charter schools had been dropped when the bell finally buzzed. Sixth period was coming. Delaney put a newspaper into his shoulder bag, and delivered what was his occasional battle cry.

"One hundred fifty kids and five shows a day," he announced matter-of-factly, using his fingers to sponge up a few dessert crumbs before walking toward the lounge's door. From my perspective, Delaney seemed as excited to take center stage in a Mount Pleasant classroom as he might have been to work on an assembly line.

Shortly after the teachers dragged themselves to their sixth-period classes, I went home, rolled up my sleeves, and sat at my cramped desk. I had schoolwork to do, too. But not for Mount Pleasant.

I turned on my laptop, and opened a seventy-one-page draft of a document for the umpteenth time. It was titled "Building Charter School Capacity in California." I'd cowritten it over the previous few months, with the conviction that it would become a major contribution to the state's charter school movement. I saw the report as having a positive influence on nearly every person connected with the state's public schools.

I liked to think that the report could have such an impact someday, anyway. The document wasn't yet finished, as evidenced by my overstuffed e-mail inbox. The burgeoning inbox was a reminder that I was attempting something very ambitious: trying to please all of the charter school constituents all of the time.

The letters in my inbox generally hailed from three groups of concerned and passionate individuals, all of whom had seen prior drafts of the report. These people were at the center of California's then ten-year-old charter school movement. One group consisted of those folks running the four hundred or so California charter schools then in existence; another group worked at the umbrella organizations supporting California's charter schools; and the third group was made up of the decision makers at some of the biggest philanthropies in the nation, including the Bill & Melinda Gates Foundation, the Walton Family Foundation (associated with Wal-Mart), and the Pisces Foundation (associated with Gap Inc.). Such organizations are longtime major funders and driving forces in the U.S. charter school movement.

Tension existed between the three groups because the report proposed to "build capacity," so to speak, through the formation of what would be the country's then largest charter school umbrella organization. There was potential for such an organization to offer major advantages to the state's charter school movement: improved academic accountability and political advocacy, plus expansion via the opening of brand-new charter schools. But the three interest groups had intense and often conflicting desires regarding the birth and structure of such an organization. They also questioned its goals.

Looking at the e-mails, I knew I could tackle only one inquiry at a time. Among letters titled "Out with the Old" and "Whose Board Is This, Anyway?" I opened an e-mail with a subject line that said, "10 in 10: Why Does This Matter?"

The writer represented a major charitable foundation. "This figure you've proposed, that the charter schools enroll 10 percent of California primary and secondary public school students within ten years? Isn't it somewhat off-point?" he'd written. "You're thinking *quantity* when the movement should focus on *quality*. Would 5 percent growth be considered a failure? Does 13 percent growth mean that the state's charter school movement is an unquestioned success?"

I scrolled through the report, looking for where I'd mentioned the "10 in 10" concept (I could swear it was on page 28). While the cursor made its way down the document, I glanced at the ever-present picture of Nolan Ryan just to the left of my desk.

There was the iconic pitcher, poised on the mound, complete with his face freshly gashed by a batted ball. The image had me asking myself if I'd emerge from this melee otherwise known as the charter school movement without tasting my own blood.

Maybe not. I'd first come to understand the depth of dissension that existed within the movement only three months earlier. Back in February, Reed Hastings had invited me to a meeting in San Francisco. Representatives from the three concerned parties would all be present to discuss the state of the state's charter schools.

Before I attended, Hastings explained to me that the movement's major funders (including Hastings himself) had already contributed tens of millions of dollars to the California charter school movement. Substantial monies had been poured into the California Network of Educational Charters (CANEC).

Despite all the contributions, CANEC, which at the time was the state's biggest charter school umbrella organization, wasn't lobbying effectively in state politics. Also, some charter schools associated with CANEC were underperforming academically. Hastings knew academic advancement wasn't the only way in which children progress and grow. But he also was aware that academic achievement was the one metric used for comparison by all California public schools.

Hastings added that while CANEC didn't necessarily oppose change, there were still plenty of people associated with the organization and the movement who wanted charter schools to be defined as *alternative* public schools. Schools, Hastings said, that would use funders' and taxpayers' money but not necessarily strive academically. To him, academic apathy was unacceptable.

Okay, I'd thought to myself as I walked into the meeting, held inside the sprawling San Francisco boardroom of Gap Inc. on a cool afternoon in February. This ought to be a lively debate.

But it was more like walking in on the Hatfields and the McCoys. There were moments of calm, and many others of near fury. I remember that those in the room representing the funders generally wore pressed shirts and pants. Those associated with CANEC and charter schools generally wore jeans and T-shirts.

Many of those wearing pressed shirts wanted change and accountability. Plenty of people in T-shirts wanted to retain the alternative-school spirit.

The pressed shirts wanted evolution or even the replacement of CANEC.

The T-shirts didn't want the funders calling all the shots.

The pressed shirts complained that they might very well be pouring money down a hole.

When the pressed shirts and the T-shirts finally agreed that California's charter school movement needed direction and a detailed road map going forward, the call went out for volunteers to generate a strategic plan. Only a few hands went up. One was mine.

I was aware that the project would be a lot of work. I also believed that if the plan were properly executed, it could be enormously influential, beneficial, and even personally fulfilling. I'd already had a very positive and satisfying experience many years before in taking up a huge social cause.

I once joined several other people in a gigantic legal showdown against the then quarter-million-member-strong Jaycees. That's right:

the very same organization that originally brought Carol and me together.

The only reason the two of us ever overlapped in the Jaycees was because its Palo Alto chapter was coed. But our mixed-sex chapter was an anomaly, and in violation of the Jaycees' bylaws, which at the time stated that the organization was exclusively for men.

The Jaycees' Oklahoma-based national leadership never warmed to the behavior of a certain rogue Northern California chapter (several other chapters nationwide had taken a similar mixed-sex stance). Soon after I became president of the Palo Alto chapter in 1982, I got a letter from the Jaycees' national leadership. Based on my chapter's lack of compliance with the bylaws, the national organization planned to sue us in federal court for trademark infringement. Essentially, the Jaycees wanted the Palo Alto folks out of their club.

But our modest, then fifty-person chapter didn't fold under pressure. We fought back, finding pro bono legal help, aligning with other Jaycee chapters caught in the same predicament, and appealing to the media. I was a twenty-five-year-old kid standing in front of TV cameras, microphones, and a federal courthouse, railing against what at its core was discrimination. Didn't women deserve better?

While I moved from my job at Boston Consulting Group to the launch of my first start-up company, the Jaycees case climbed through the courts. Ultimately it got bundled together with a handful of similar cases nationwide, and was put in front of the United States Supreme Court. In 1984, the court voted overwhelmingly in our favor. The Jaycees had to change their bylaws to accept women.

I don't want to beat my chest too loudly, but I will say that the Supreme Court's ruling against the Jaycees was historic. Other huge national organizations, such as the Rotary, Kiwanis, and Lions clubs, were ultimately forced to follow suit. The decision represented a gigantic victory for women's rights, and was one of my proudest moments.

So yes, I knew there would be a lot of work and potential struggle when I raised my hand to help the state's charter school movement in that Gap boardroom. I'd wanted to do the work of writing the strategic plan—for charter schools specifically and public schools in general. California's students deserved better. In fact, one of the first lines I wrote in the new report stated, "We recommend charters because we think that when they succeed, they can spur widespread improvements across the system."

If only the rest of the project had come so easily. Cowriting the report with two colleagues—one was the principal of an academically rigorous San Francisco charter school, the other a longtime CANEC board member—made for a lot of stormy moments. Heads frequently butted.

Following the first month of work, we decided to fold CANEC into a new organization, steered by a board of directors that represented the interests of all the major players in the state's charter school movement. The organization would have new executive leadership, provide more advocacy for the state's charter school movement, and hold its member schools accountable for their academics. The new organization would also emphasize expansion by facilitating the launch of new charter schools until their numbers reached "critical mass."

Ever since I was lectured by SnapTrack's board of directors into thinking of ways to capture the widest possible audience, I have paid great attention to the concept of critical mass. *Critical mass* can be loosely defined as the threshold at which an idea, a phenomenon, or even a product takes on self-sustaining momentum. In terms of incorporating locator technology into cell phones, I would argue that critical mass was achieved when the Federal Communications Commission recognized that such a technology could save many lives. The question at the FCC became, why *wouldn't* all cell phones have that type of innovation? Luckily for me and for all the others at SnapTrack, we developed an industry-leading locator technology, and a big company decided to squeeze our invention into as many cell phones as possible.

In terms of the threshold at which changes occur in traditional schools, a former Harvard economics professor who studied the subject estimated that critical mass for charter schools and other "schools of choice" (as in magnet and private schools) could be reached at approximately 10 percent enrollment (the figure itself comes from economics theory). That is, when schools of choice command about 10 percent of a given area's total school enrollment, their educational strategies gain momentum, while the student populations and potential government monies simultaneously get siphoned away from traditional schools. In turn, those traditional schools must respond with change.

What might such change look like? Perhaps traditional schools would adopt some of the characteristics of successful charter schools: teachers and principals obtaining the freedom to work more collaboratively, making their own choices regarding their budgets and teaching materials, and receiving increased pay for producing more high-achieving students. Recent test scores and research—from California and other states—indicate that charter schools are indeed helping to close the achievement gap between poor and wealthier schools. The question isn't whether or not charter schools will take over, because they won't. The movement is still tiny. But that doesn't mean that good, lean, and mean charter schools can't prove the value of, say, local control of classrooms. Perhaps California's state legislature, for example, might notice increasing numbers of cases of charter school success, and give real consideration to the idea of greatly empowering *all* of its traditional public schools.

Which brings me back to the "10 in 10" statistic that I was looking for while sitting at my desk on that same late May day when Delaney had insisted that I wanted to privatize public schools. He was wrong. I didn't. I kept the new organization's suggested target goal—10 percent of all California public school students enrolled in charter schools within ten years—in the plan because I wanted to do whatever I could to increase the chances that California's entire public education system would improve. I felt like *quantity* of the charter schools had to be about as important to the charter school movement as *quality*.

"Building Charter School Capacity in California" ultimately became the blueprint for the organization that today is known as the California Charter Schools Association. I served as the association's first chairman of the board, and among the CCSA's many accomplishments, I'm proud to say, has been strong growth: Today there are approximately eight hundred charter schools in California, or double what there were back when I helped create the report. The 400,000 students in those charter schools would, if taken together, represent the fifth-largest school district in the nation.

For once, I was the guy in my American Government class watching the clock. It was two days after debating my charter school efforts with Delaney, and I impatiently waited for my students to leave the classroom after the bell sounded. I was eager to lock up behind them. My plan was to skip lunch in the lounge and drive to one of the worst neighborhoods in Oakland. I wanted to see what the future of California public school education might look like.

Lionel Wilson College Preparatory Academy is a sixth- through twelfth-grade school in south Oakland, not far from the airport, freeway, and railroad tracks, in one of the town's most miserable neighborhoods. One Web site warns that the area "has a very high crime rate . . . you will get jacked if your ass gets lost in there at night."

Luckily I visited Wilson Prep during the day. The school, which wasn't far from a wall covered in graffiti and an empty lot dotted with wind-blown trash, resembled nothing short of an unblemished oasis. The buildings featured silvery corrugated metal paneling, and the main structure's design was crisp and modern. The front doors were painted a sunny yellow, and felt welcoming.

"There's a lot of pride here," said Troyvoi Hicks, the dreadlocked school principal, who greeted me soon after my arrival and took me on a tour of the school. "I'm hopeful for great things from the place."

He wasn't the only one. Wilson Prep, which at the time I visited was in its first year of operation, came about through the efforts of many people. To me, the school was a prototype for what could be done when the charter school movement fires on all cylinders.

Central to Wilson Prep's launch was a nonprofit organization called Aspire Public Schools, and its founder, Don Shalvey. Aspire is a charter management organization (CMO) that's focused on doing all that's needed to open charter schools and have them thrive.

In the case of Wilson Prep, Aspire had to petition for local support to open a school, secure the land, build the building, hire a staff, and create a curriculum. And that was just for starters. The advantage of a CMO like Aspire over even the most energetic individual or group attempting to launch a charter school is in its experience and systematization of practices. How big a feat was opening Wilson Prep? It was the first new public high school building constructed in Oakland in the last forty years.

Aspire's biggest asset at the time was arguably Shalvey himself. When Wilson Prep opened, Shalvey was only a couple of years out of his longtime job as a Bay Area school superintendent. Shalvey had already been at the charter school game since 1992, when he squeezed in enough time and work to open the first such school in the state. He had launched Aspire's first charter school in 1999, on a shoestring, in the former space of a grocery store in a strip mall in the humble central California town of Modesto. Thus Lionel Wilson Prep represented progress for Shalvey, too: He'd secured generous donations from benefactors like the Bill & Melinda Gates and Walton Family foundations and those monies were absolutely critical for Aspire's ability to build the new school. As it turned out such high-profile philanthropies were more than willing to open their wallets for someone that they knew would get the job done.

I was fortunate enough to know Shalvey's inspirational energy firsthand. The same *Journal* story that had encouraged me to pick the brain of Reed Hastings did the same with regard to Shalvey. The newspaper had called Shalvey an "education entrepreneur," which immediately made him my kind of guy. I contacted him soon after reading the piece, and we quickly struck up a friendship.

Shalvey taught me a lot of what I know about charter schools, and I gave him some business pointers. Even before I started working at Mount Pleasant, I began serving on Aspire's board of directors. In the end, however, I think our relationship has benefited me the most. I don't know that I would have ever known the potential for the future of California's public education without sitting at the feet of the forever forward-thinking Shalvey. When we talked on the phone a couple of weeks before my visit to Wilson Prep, Shalvey told me, "When you go there, remember that we're educating the kids for their future. Not our past."

Touring Wilson Prep with Hicks, I walked around a school that, sure enough, was very different from the schools I'd attended in Houston. It was very different from Mount Pleasant.

For instance, shortly after I arrived, we walked past the "Yale" classroom. All the classrooms are named after colleges instead of numbered, and for a good reason: The expectation is that every one of Wilson Prep's students, despite the vast majority of them being socio-economically disadvantaged, will graduate and go on to a four-year college. In one of the classrooms, Hicks asked three Hispanic boys a question. "College?" he said, and they immediately responded: *"Claro!"* (Of course!)

In pursuit of that goal, Hicks explained, the Wilson Prep students spend about 15 percent more time in class than other public school kids. Wilson Prep's school year is longer, as are some of the high school students' classes. The school's two-hour classes, for example, were designed to take the kids deep into the subject matter.

"We have a culture," Hicks told me toward the end of my visit, "that consistently stresses that kids can and should learn."

The next day at Mount Pleasant, I felt the sensation of having brought at least a whiff of Hicks's attitude into my own class. Five minutes before the period ended, I gave the students their graded civil rights papers. I was excited. Almost everyone, from Joe to Moe to Tracy, had made significant improvements in their writing over the course of the semester.

These final homework papers were proof of the students' progress. The thesis statements were stronger, and the supporting arguments beefier. Some kids even wrote transitions and infused humor. Plus nobody turned in the kind of three-sentence efforts that I'd received at the beginning of the semester.

After distributing all of them, I leaned against the teacher's desk, crossed my arms, and smiled.

"Congratulations. You guys did great!" I said. "By improving your writing, you've really accomplished something."

I saw Komal's eyes move across her paper's front page, and could only assume that she was reading my compliments and encouragement. She cracked a little smile. Other kids in the class showed one another their grades while speaking quietly. Jimmy and Pete, however, were not so subtle.

"Something else we accomplished, bro," said Jimmy, holding up his hand to high-five Pete. "The last paper we may *ever* have to write."

Tracy, meanwhile, was too busy braiding her hair and talking to a friend to notice that I'd given her a straight A. Her writing was nearly flawless.

But I wasn't about to dwell on apathy today. Like Troyvoi Hicks, I believed that kids can and should learn. And I felt like I had taught almost all of my students at least a few solid lessons about writing.

Soon class ended, and Joe approached my desk. He had a look of happy disbelief.

"What's up, Joe? Hey, great job on the paper," I said.

"Mr. Poizner," said Reardon, with a big smile on his long face. "I'm pumped! An A."

"You built a compelling argument, paragraph by paragraph," I said. "Remember how your earliest homework was just a bunch of jumbled sentences? You deserve this."

"I guess I did earn it," he said humbly, and just kept staring at the high mark.

Joe was unquestionably my most improved student, and a few days later I'd praise him for that progress, too. In fact, I'd announce his accomplishment to the entire class.

Joe had begun American Government as the student with an asterisk, a special-education kid with dyslexia who might require additional help. But the asterisk by his name at the end of the semester represented something completely different. Earlier, Purcell had asked all of his teachers to recognize one student in each class that had made the most progress during the semester. For me, picking Joe was a no-brainer.

I didn't often get the feeling that I was greatly empowering my Mount Pleasant students. They were frequently cynical, preoccupied, or indifferent. But I thought I really had an effect on Joe, in a way that usually only happens for teachers in the movies.

I'd called them again—Mrs. Cardenas, Mr. Saldanha, Mrs. Vega, and the rest of my students' parents—with the hopes that they'd come to the Parents' Night that I'd scheduled for early June. I'd come to the conclusion that the event might be my only opportunity to meet any of them.

As one might guess, parent involvement at a charter school is often very hands-on. In a charter school, parents could be volunteering in the classroom, coaching a school sports team, or working on the school's teacher-hiring committee.

At Wilson Prep, for example, parents must attend special Saturday classes with their children to keep abreast of the subject matter. Parents can also receive coaching on the best ways to help kids with their homework. Plus, at the start of each school year, Wilson Prep parents must sign on one of the lines of what is a three-way school-family-student compact. The compact carefully spells out what's expected of all the parties. It's like the MOU that I'd given my Mount Pleasant students back in January, but on steroids. Wilson Prep calls each participant in the compact a "stakeholder."

Research consistently shows that parent involvement in their kids' educations—whether it's manning the barbecue at a school fair or working on a parent-teacher board—reaps report-card rewards.

Knowing that, I was hopeful that even one parent visit to the school might have a positive effect on my students. What if I lit a fire under the parent of one of my kids who was almost failing? What if some of the parents' enthusiasm rubbed off? What if a student studied a little harder for the final, or reviewed her PowerPoint presentation just one more time? Going into the last couple weeks of the semester, I was the schoolteacher version of a race car mechanic: I entertained any idea that might up the kids' performance.

I had another motive for hosting a Parents' Night, too. I thought the parents should know what was possible in a classroom. My peers had neither my resources nor the luxury of funneling all their energies into one class. But what if other teachers had even a fraction of the resources or time that I had? What if schools had smaller class sizes and better access to foundation money? Without sounding arrogant, I wanted my kids' parents to get a glimpse of what school could be like. Maybe learning about what took place in my American Government class would motivate the parents to demand more from the education of a younger son or daughter. Or to ask the graduating (I could only hope!) high school senior in the house how he or she might take further advantage of any lessons learned during that last semester of school.

On a warm Thursday evening, a modest group of adults trickled into another one of Mount Pleasant's humble teachers' lounges for the meeting. The parents appeared a lot like their kids, in sweats and T-shirts, or jeans and casual short-sleeved shirts, with sunglasses propped on their heads. A few opted to grab some dessert—I'd bought cookies and Häagen-Dazs ice cream bars for anyone who was interested. I took a quick head count. There were about fifteen parents in all. Not great, but not horrible. I figured there was one adult in the room to represent every other one of my students.

"Hello, and thanks for coming to twelfth-grade American Government's Parents' Night," I said from the front of the room, facing the adults and my students, who were seated together in rows of chairs. There was a man sitting next to Pete who looked like he could be Pete's dad. Tracy and Jimmy were both sitting next to adults, too.

"There are notepads and pens next to the ice cream bars," I continued, with a wave of my right hand. "The test at the end will be part essay, part multiple choice."

I got a few gratuitous chuckles, which reminded me of my first day in front of my American Government class. Nobody laughed at my jokes then, either.

"No, seriously, we've done a lot of great stuff this semester," I quickly added, feeling the need to keep things moving. "We've learned about constitutional rights and voter behavior. We've heard oral arguments during a field trip to San Francisco's U.S. Court of Appeals for the Ninth Circuit and listened to FBI agents talk about terrorism."

I saw a few heads nod in confirmation and gave the floor to the evening's guest speaker. I'd asked Reed Hastings to come say a few words, and introduced him as the president of the California State Board of Education. Hastings gave a brief, heartfelt speech about academic performance and his determination to improve it across the state.

He received a polite round of applause.

Then I nodded for Tracy to come to the front of the room.

"I'm Tracy Cardenas, and that's my mom and little brother," she said, pointing to a woman wearing a blue Nike T-shirt and holding a cute little boy in her right arm.

Tracy and I glanced at each other, and I clicked on a PowerPoint slide on my laptop. The image projected onto a pull-down screen.

"One of my favorite things we did was hear a debate for and against the death penalty from two experts with totally different perspectives," said Tracy, reading the slide. "Did you know that it costs more money to execute someone than it does to have him serve a life sentence in prison?" she said. "Also, lots of people debate whether or not the death penalty deters crime."

Tracy sat down, and to my surprise nobody clapped except her mom. Then a boy from my class got up to explain who Richard Clarke was, and that I'd worked for him in the White House, and that he'd visited the school one day and talked about his attempts to find Osama bin Laden.

The room remained quiet. When a few of my students stood up to talk about their Close Up trip to Washington, D.C., I got up from behind my laptop and walked over to Purcell. He was standing at the back of the room.

"Why isn't anyone applauding for anything we've done? I think we're talking about some good moments," I whispered.

He leaned toward me.

"Maybe some of the parents are a little intimidated," he said. "All these names and titles. It's not too often that we get visits from terrorist czars and hear speeches made by the president of California's State Board of Education. The folks here are probably wondering what planet you came from."

Just then a man with a shaved head who was wearing a Subway T-shirt raised his hand. It was the first question of the night. One of the kids who was standing and talking about visiting the Vietnam Veterans Memorial paused. He pointed to the inquisitive parent.

"I didn't know my kid went to Washington, D.C.," the man said.

The man's son was right next to him, and rolled his eyes. Then he whispered loudly, "Dad, that was only some people. I didn't go."

Everyone finally had a good laugh.

After the meeting ended, I shook the parents' hands and stole bites of an ice cream bar.

"Maybe when this one is old enough," said Mrs. Cardenas, pointing to the little boy wrapped over her shoulder and asleep, "I can send him on the Close Up trip. Tracy says she hates all the papers. But I know she appreciates you paying so much attention. Thank you."

Behind Mrs. Cardenas was a woman with soft, big brown eyes who didn't look nearly as angry as the young man who I figured was her son. Otherwise it was obvious that she and Jimmy were related.

"I'm Mrs. Vega. Jimmy's mom," she said, and looked over her shoulder. Jimmy was by the desserts, not saying much and grimacing. Apparently he had little interest in spending an evening at school.

"I know that he's missed a lot of classes, Mr. Poizner," she said. "Do you think he'll pass?"

"Well, that's my hope," I said softly. "I want him to pass. Can you encourage him to study for next week's final? And to practice his PowerPoint presentation?"

"Maybe I can push some, Mr. Poizner," she said.

"Have him practice that presentation," I said. "Jimmy's tentative in front of a crowd. He can't skip that presentation."

Mrs. Vega said okay.

Pete walked up behind her.

"Mr. Poizner, this is my dad, Enrique Franco."

"Hi, Mr. Franco," I said, shaking his hand.

"*Mucho gusto*," he said.

Mr. Franco was short, with uneven teeth, a three-day beard, and thick calluses on his palms. His face was tan to the point of being sun-baked. Did Mr. Franco work outside? He and Pete had the same friendly smile.

"I speak a little English, Mr. Poizner," said Mr. Franco.

We had a simple conversation. And then Mr. Franco lightly grabbed my arm.

"Keep trying with Pete," he said, his eyes surrounded by pronounced lines in his skin. "I don't understand Pete's books. It's not easy. Please keep trying."

I nodded.

"Usted tiene suerte para tener un maestro como él," Mr. Franco said to Pete.

Pete turned to me. "He said I'm lucky to have a teacher like you."

I humbly thanked Mr. Franco and told him that Pete had a lot of teachers who tried. He and his son soon left.

Pete was within a hair's width of failing American Government. So was Jimmy.

I'd fail the boys if they deserved to fail. And I'd hate doing it. Call me a sucker for the concerned mom or dad, or a rookie teacher with heartstrings just waiting to be tugged. But meeting Jimmy's worried mom and Pete's hopeful father, even though we were at the semester's eleventh hour, caused me some inner turmoil. I quickly felt like they were parents who didn't deserve for their kids to flunk.

Was I foolish to let in such feelings? Which students enjoyed good role models? Who had parents with horrible habits? Of course it was impossible to tell over a brief presentation, a handshake, and some ice cream. But I still believed that the parents I met wanted their children to succeed, and just may not have known how to pursue that success. I felt like any school should do what it could to work with an anxious mom, or to come to the aid of a father whose best intentions for his son were literally lost in translation.

We were at the semester's end. Next week was our class trip to San Jose's City Hall and the PowerPoint presentations. After that came the final. Graduation was the following week.

Jimmy and Pete, along with a couple of other students in the class, had to pass the final and do a decent job on their presentations to avoid failing. Komal and Tracy were both going to pass, unless disaster struck. The suspense around Joe was whether or not he'd pull an A. He was close.

Where would these seniors have been at this point of the semester in a college-oriented charter high school? Maybe Jimmy and Pete would have failed long ago.

Maybe they'd be thriving. Rigorous charter schools, which have zero patience for students' excuses and expect the kids to try very hard, work on developing focus and a sense of responsibility. Oakland's Wilson Prep, for instance, puts each of its high school students into small, adult-led advisory groups. The groups meet daily to provide their members with structure, guidance, and encouragement.

We didn't have advisory groups at Mount Pleasant. There was no overarching expectation that the seniors would be studying hard for their last tests, let alone anticipating a coming fall semester as a freshman at a four-year college.

But my American Government class had something that the charter schools didn't: *Jeopardy!*

Between feeling repulsed by the notion of my students failing and the resignation that I couldn't overhaul their expectations or behavior, I'd squeezed my brain to figure out how I could get the kids to cram. My best idea: a game.

I'd already gone to a hobby store and picked up a rudimentary setup of buttons, wires, and lights that would allow us to play Jeopardy. On the last Friday of regular classes, I walked into room 612 with the Jeopardy equipment packed inside a cardboard box.

"What's in there?" said Moe, walking over to my desk, where I'd set down the box. "End-of-semester cake?"

"No, Moe. Not a cake," I said. "Let's wait until everyone gets here. I'll explain."

When the room filled and the door closed, I asked if anyone wanted to play a game.

"On the last day of class?" said Pete. His eyes moved from side to side, like we were all about to get away with something sneaky. "Sure!"

"Shouldn't we be reviewing for the test?" asked Tracy.

I almost fell over. She wanted to *study*?

"This will be review," I said, and saw Pete's smile flatten. "I think it'll also be fun."

I opened the box and explained how we'd play. Eight students at a time would sit at eight designated desks. Each of those desks would get a box with a button on it, and the bigger box on my desk, which was wired to the eight small boxes, would indicate which participant had pressed their button first. A participant could press the button only when he or she was ready to respond.

"Like on *Jeopardy!*, I'll give you clues and hints in the form of an answer," I said, and told the kids to give me their answers formed as questions.

"Duh," said Moe. "It's the same way on television."

The kids would earn a point for a correct answer, and lose a point for an incorrect answer. The three people with the most points would win some Mars candy bars.

Eight kids sat at the designated desks. All the others stood or sat at the remaining desks.

"Okay, question one," I said, reading from a list of prepared questions. "They're collectively known as the Constitution's first ten amendments."

After about five seconds, the number 4 light lit up on my box. The contestant was Antonio Boras. The kid next to him pounded his fist on his desk, frustrated because he apparently pressed his button a nanosecond too late.

"What is the Bill of Rights?" asked Boras.

"Correct," I said.

"Next question," I said. "The dominant form of United States politics . . ."

The number 6 light lit up before I could finish. The contestant was Komal.

Two other participants moaned for not being faster with their fingers.

"The Republicans!" she said.

"No," I said. "Let me read the entire question. It's the dominant form of United States politics, and includes both the Democrats and the Republicans."

None of my lights flashed.

"Oh, I *so* know the answer to this," said Donny Mates from the back of the room.

Finally the number 3 light blinked on. The contestant was a girl named Audrey Valverde.

"What is the electoral system?" she shouted with a big grin.

"Sorry," I said.

Donny moaned. Tracy Cardenas was dying to throw out an answer, too. But it wasn't her turn to play.

The number 1 light came on. Jimmy.

"What is the two-party system?" he said tentatively.

That's the hard thing about being a tough guy, I thought. You're afraid to be wrong.

"Yes!" I said.

After a few more questions, I rotated another eight kids into the game. They were eager to play. The current round of participants, how-ever, didn't want to stop. Everyone's enthusiasm kept building to the point where the kids who weren't playing were jumping out of their desks to crowd around the eight contestants. Every exchange brought on more yells, fist pumps, and hyperbolic groans. At one point Donny correctly answered a tough question about the Fourth Amendment, and jumped on top of his desk. I was quickly losing control of the class.

A few minutes later Wald opened the door to the room and peeked in, only to see the whooping and hollering. When he approached me from across the room, the students didn't stop.

"What's going on?" he said, his eyes open wide, his hands on his waist.

"Yeah, sorry. We're playing this Jeopardy game, using class mate-rial," I said apologetically. "I'm having a hard time maintaining calm."

Wald stuck around for a couple of rounds. The students couldn't be contained. I was embarrassed.

"Steve," Wald said to me in a loud voice, trying to talk over the din. Then he leaned forward to get closer so that he didn't have to scream.

"This is excellent," he said, with a small nod. "They're into it."

We played for the entire period. Moe and Tracy earned Mars bars. Komal ended up with negative points, courtesy of her extremely itchy trigger finger. But in the end, she was smiling. Donny had broken a sweat. Pete and Jimmy both got a couple of points.

During the game, I'd asked something related to virtually every question that was on the upcoming final. We'd covered a staggering amount of subject matter. The kids had, in a weird way, focused as perhaps I'd never seen them focus.

Were my methods truly effective? I didn't know. Of course I wanted my students to be perfectly prepared for what was coming. But if that wasn't possible, at least I had them learning right up to the very end.

CHAPTER 9

Graduation Day Arrives

W arren Buffett once told me that I took crazy chances.
Years ago, I got the rare opportunity to visit Buffett,
the now seventy-nine-year-old, famously successful
businessman and investor, in his Omaha, Nebraska, office. We talked
about things unrelated to education or technology. He also wanted to
know about my past, and Buffett listened intently as I explained all
the trials and tribulations I had encountered in turning SnapTrack
from a hazy concept into a billion-dollar business. He raised a bushy
eyebrow.

"So many risks. The technology, the patents, working with the government," he said with good-natured sincerity. "Too complicated and
unpredictable. I would have never invested in your company."

As a businessman or an investor, I don't pretend to be in Buffett's
league. But it's not like the "Oracle of Omaha" hasn't taken a chance
or three during his prolific career. So it was instructive to know that a

guy like Buffett wouldn't have touched SnapTrack with a ten-foot pole. I guess I really do love risk.

Buffett undoubtedly would have rolled his eyes if he'd been with me on a Monday morning in early June 2003. I stood alone in front of a rented bus, in the parking lot of Mount Pleasant High School. My students were late to meet me for our trip to San Jose's City Hall, and I was starting to wonder if they were going to show up at all. I'd bet big that they would: The success of my entire semester of teaching hinged on my students delivering PowerPoint presentations to the mayor of San Jose.

Standing idle in that parking lot gave me time to get anxious, and to wonder if my risk taking—no matter my calculations and convictions—occasionally did border on crazy.

Giving PowerPoint presentations to the mayor of San Jose would have been a big deal for any group of students, let alone one coming from a public high school in a struggling community. Outside of what my students had experienced in our class, most of the kids had no history of mixing with people of power or authority, especially in close contact, as if they were peers.

Couldn't I have just given a final exam like all the other teachers, I thought to myself, looking at my watch. I had to be different. I had to try something extraordinary.

From the start, the community engagement projects had elicited moans and groans from the students. Some had told me that they'd enjoyed the data collection, which often meant interacting with schoolmates and friends. But none of the kids declared that they were eager to narrate their findings.

We had a dress rehearsal of the PowerPoint presentations a week earlier. The dry run had gone just okay. Pete had signed up another dozen or so people in his voter registration drive, putting his tally at an almost respectable forty signatures. Tracy had fielded a decent number of opinions about abortion, but her group's presentation had been disorganized. Jimmy continued to mumble in front of an audience, and he wasn't the only one.

What if, I thought while leaning against the bus, some of the kids just said, "Screw it"? Jimmy had cut a handful of American Government classes already. Sure, he'd need a high school diploma to become a marine. But maybe, he might be thinking, he could finish up in summer school.

And Pete? His dad's wishes were his dad's. I had pushed Pete to get those last signatures. I had repeatedly encouraged him to set up his voter registration table in front of a supermarket, grab a clipboard, and try talking to people one last time. I'd thought about his dad urging me to stay on his son. But what if Pete had woken up this morning, smiled, shrugged, and went to the movies?

What if Komal's dad up and moved her over the weekend?

What if Moe was rude to the mayor?

Was that battle-ax of a San Jose high school bureaucrat right, the one who nine months ago rejected my offer to volunteer in her school system? Had I ever belonged in the classroom?

What had I asked these students to do?

Then, from around a corner of the bus, Joe appeared. So did Donny and Moe. Tracy and Jimmy. Komal wasn't far behind, ditto Pete and Audrey. All thirty-two of my students showed up, and I was grateful enough to envision prostrating myself in gratitude. They were willing to take on risk, too. And they wanted to graduate.

"You've got the ambitious ones"—that's what Wald had once told me. As we all loaded onto the bus, I finally saw the truth in that comment.

· · ·

The trip to what was then San Jose's City Hall, a glass-sided, Eisenhower-era, unadorned structure, was unlike the class's previous bus rides. There was none of the banter and laughing that I'd heard on other field trips. Those bus rides had represented escape and exploration. This field trip was about challenge and facing fear. The mayor was waiting. I barely heard a peep during the fifteen-minute drive.

The students all filed into a meeting room in City Hall's fourth floor. We drew the blinds, wired my laptop to a projector, and pulled down a screen. Tracy and Komal shared a timid laugh about something. Moe had a brief conversation with Pete.

Then Mayor Ron Gonzales and City Councilwoman Nora Campos walked into the room, and the place went silent. The mayor, straight-backed and square-jawed, looked regal in his blue blazer and red and blue tie. His hair was smoothed back like a movie star's. His eyes searched out others' eyes. As if Mayor Gonzales needed to seem even more important, one of his aides fussed endlessly by his side.

Gonzales finally sat down at the end of a long conference table, like a king in his court.

The students all stared at him. I wondered if they were breathing.

I took a deep breath myself.

"Mayor Gonzales, Councilwoman Campos, thanks for hosting us today. We're honored," I said.

I introduced myself and the class.

"Earlier in the semester, the students split into teams to tackle what we call community engagement projects," I continued. "Each team identified a problem in the community and wanted to address it.

"Through our studies, we've discovered how issues can be tackled via a political process," I added. "My twelfth-grade students thought what they've studied should be called to your attention. They thought increased awareness was a solid first step toward coming up with solutions."

"Sounds very good," said Mayor Gonzales, adjusting his glasses as if to fine-tune his already sharp focus. "Let's hear what people discovered."

I turned toward the kids. They looked stiff.

I felt like a drama teacher about to watch my students play victims in some modern adaptation of *Henry VIII*.

"Moe, start us off," I said. "What did your group address? What did you find?"

I had thought Moe's motormouth and cravings for attention were made for this moment. A couple of weeks ago, I'd apologized to him for my previous outburst. Then I'd asked Moe to lead off in the presentations delivered to the mayor. He'd been honored and excited.

But that was then, and this was crunch time.

Moe stood up and tapped on the laptop. A slide came up on the screen. He looked at Mayor Gonzales.

"Well, you know," said Moe. "We . . ."

Uh-oh, I thought.

"Well, we kinda started . . ." he added, and then said nothing.

"We did this survey," he said, pulling at his shirt collar, as if it were kinking his windpipe.

Come on, Moe, I thought. Keep it together. Don't lose your nerve.

"We wanted to find out what students thought of U.S. foreign policy," he finally said. "We asked more than two hundred Mount Pleasant social sciences students what they thought of our country's actions abroad, and how that affected their lives back in San Jose," said Moe, now speaking nervously and fast. "We thought maybe events happening on the other sides of our borders were affecting us like, um, at home," he said. "I mean, politicians should know that what they decide to do about faraway problems might make people in local neighborhoods feel really good or totally bad."

Moe tapped on the laptop. Another slide came up, with six pie charts.

"Now Audrey will interpret the results," he added and happily fell into his chair.

Audrey Valverde explained that most of the polled students were against war. She said that they couldn't understand why peace was so elusive. Polled students also felt strongly that the United States needed to do more to stop world hunger. Plus the country's immigration policies left many of the survey participants wanting.

"Mount Pleasant students don't understand why the United States has such mixed reactions about immigrants," she said. "The kids we talked to said that the country was built by immigrants. Why do they get a bad deal sometimes now?"

"An important question," said the mayor, sitting back in his seat. "People like us in government, especially here in California, come up against immigration issues constantly," he added. "We'll continue to work on them. But your voice should be heard, too. You guys—your generation—will make many important immigration-related decisions for this country."

Then the mayor smiled. "Nice presentation," he said.

Pete's group was next.

"We, uh . . ." Pete said, running a hand through his hair.

There was an uncomfortably long pause.

"We worked with the general public to . . ."

Not again, I thought. You can do this, Pete.

"We recognized that there's a problem with voters," Pete said.

"What's the problem?" said Mayor Gonzales, leaning forward over the conference table.

"There aren't enough of them," said Pete.

The mayor nodded.

"More people should register to vote," Pete added. "Not enough people vote."

He explained his difficulties with registering people. The people he approached didn't always want to give him attention.

"Why do you think folks avoided you?" asked Mayor Gonzales. "Why wouldn't they care about voting?"

Franco froze for what seemed like a long time. I couldn't stand seeing him so tied up.

"Pete, do you remember how we talked about . . ." I interjected.

But Pete interrupted me. He had collected himself.

"People don't think they can make a difference. Casting one vote, they think, man, that won't do anything! People think they're too busy to vote, too," he said. "They don't see that voting is a gift. Like, not everyone in the world gets to vote. I kept saying to people I tried to sign up, hey, this is an opportunity to make things happen. Races can be really close."

The mayor crossed his arms and nodded. Pete happily gave up the floor to another member of his group.

The presentations continued, each student willing him- or herself to stand up and speak to the mayor for two or three minutes.

Nobody had an easy time of it. Donny, dressed in a screaming-red NFL jersey and blue jeans, lost some of his cool when he found that his PowerPoint slides were out of order. Komal got confused. She kept mentioning the school's "no-tardy policy" until Councilwoman Campos asked if Mount Pleasant really had zero tolerance for tardiness.

"Was that what I've been saying? I meant the school's no-hat policy," Komal said with a tense giggle.

Joe resorted to reading his slides verbatim, which, considering his dyslexia, was a battle. Tracy kept licking her lips—classic dry-mouth nervousness.

After hearing about two-thirds of the students speak, I couldn't stop smiling. I was proud. I no longer heard the mistakes or dwelled on the holes in the students' research or the seams in their execution. I saw only my kids putting themselves out there, dragging their chins up to look at the mayor and councilwoman, trying to speak with some authority about problems that affected them and their communities. Purcell was right in telling me earlier that when it came to these projects, I shouldn't seek perfection. The students were gathering their wits and all of their nerve to make the presentations at all. The efforts were exceptional.

I wished that the presentations could have gone on all day. Aside from administering the final, this was the last time I'd be with all of my students in one room. And because I wasn't teaching, or preoccupied with keeping everyone's attention, I had a moment to sit back and inventory the previous six months. The memories of the semester played back in my head in one schmaltzy highlight reel.

Jimmy's intimidating presence. Benita Johnson telling me that her fiancé was a bank robber. Joe's growing enthusiasm for the homework. A rollicking game of Jeopardy.

I'd given the class my all, tapping into my resources, my Rolodex, and my experience. The students better understood the executive branch of government because of my memories of a year spent as a White House Fellow. They better appreciated the judicial system because we watched the three-judge panel from San Francisco's Ninth Circuit Court in action. They learned how to write because I absolutely refused to give in to their complaints. I thought the state of California would be plenty satisfied with what my Mount Pleasant students took home from a twelfth-grade American Government class.

And what did the students teach the teacher? In spite of my extensive preparation, the answers to that question couldn't be found in my lesson plans. Instead, the answers would come after six months' worth of hard work and experience in a public high school classroom. A classroom where the students at various times endured, appreciated, and forgave me. I like to think that I did as much for them.

First, my students reminded me that I am a privileged man, from a privileged world. I don't mean *privilege* only in terms of material wealth. The expectations I have for what I can accomplish in life represent privilege, too, because my goals generally lie somewhere between perfection and well beyond. I'm grateful that I have the ability and wherewithal to aim so high. I'm satisfied with all that I've done, and I'm excited to achieve much more.

What I often saw in my classroom were far lower expectations. Among my students, world-beating mind-sets and grandiose hopes would often be considered luxuries as outrageous as mansions, Porsches, and trips to Monte Carlo. Many of my Mount Pleasant kids lived in confined worlds with incremental aspirations. Their concerns sometimes ranged from completing one measly paper to having enough money for a prom to hoping that a dad would someday learn to speak English. Ironically, my big goals occasionally seemed trivial next to the kids' needs, which were more basic.

But despite my being frequently sobered, the biggest takeaway I got from my kids was the notion of *potential*. For even when Steve Poizner, a one-semester volunteer with a very curious business background, happened to strike a chord with some students, the results were amazing. Realizing that all my students had potential was an immensely satisfying—no, life-affirming—discovery: I noticed potential when the kids asked Dr. Pot insightful questions, wrote solid thesis statements, researched projects by sometimes talking to hundreds of people, and stood up in front of a big-city mayor.

At Mount Pleasant, I learned that the possibility existed for each of my students to think critically, study hard, ask questions, and find passion in schoolwork. If I could generate dribs and drabs of such positive behavior, wasn't it possible that seasoned veterans, teaching the right types of classes, could open the figurative floodgates? Even if students' home lives are compromised, shouldn't school be a place of possibility? Of outrageous hopes and goals? My students taught me that they could, when properly inspired, rise to great heights.

Thus it was only fitting, on that day in San Jose's City Hall, that Jimmy Vega was the last student to speak. Jimmy had watched all his peers address an audience. He had researched the material and come to his own conclusions. Could he succeed at something that had previously been a struggle? Could the tough guy who always made a statement with his muscles get a crowd's attention with his words?

Mayor Gonzales and Councilwoman Campos had already asked the students many questions, and offered plenty of praise. They were still engaged. Two other students from Jimmy's group had discussed the importance of child safety in the home. Jimmy's job was to wrap up his group's project, and the class presentation, with a monologue about child safety in the car.

He was wearing a plaid button-down shirt—untucked, the way a young kid would wear it after playing outside at recess. Jimmy's scalp showed a few days' worth of stubble, which softened his appearance. The scar on his right arm was covered with his sleeve. He looked down at the floor. He almost appeared innocent.

"We wanted to, you know, raise awareness about driving," Jimmy said in a barely audible voice.

He gave his nose a wipe with his right hand before stuffing that hand back in his pocket.

"I mean . . ." Jimmy paused, and then cleared his throat. "We went to the local elementary school and told kids and teachers about how kids need to be safe when they're driving with their moms and dads," he said in a continued whisper.

Mayor Gonzales and Councilwoman Campos leaned forward in their seats to better hear Jimmy.

His eyes momentarily rose up toward the screen. I think he'd forgotten it was there.

"Like, people hold their kids in the car while it's moving. They're thinking that's safe for the kid. But it's totally unsafe," he said. "Most deaths for little kids happen because they weren't . . ." Then his whisper trailed off.

"Restrained?" offered Councilwoman Campos.

"That's it," he said. "Like, car crashes are a big reason that kids die," he said in a stronger voice. "Statistically, car accidents are the number one cause of deaths for kids. The kids need to be in properly installed car seats, and car owners can go to fire stations or other places to get lessons on putting them in.

"We told people at the elementary school that they need to spread the word," he added, his voice louder.

For the first time since I'd laid eyes on Jimmy many months ago, I could clearly see a teenager caught somewhere between boyhood and becoming a man. Maybe he had an NFL player's biceps, but Jimmy was still looking for courage, confidence, and guidance. He still had to find his way, just like other high school kids.

"You know," he added with conviction, "why waste a life? That's what I said to those people at the elementary school. We should be, um, smart. You know. Give kids chances."

Having nothing more to say, and clearly happy with his performance, Jimmy sat down.

I couldn't have scripted better closing remarks.

A few days later, I graded the last of the American Government final
exams. I was sitting alone in Mount Pleasant's room 612, at the teacher's desk. I should've felt a huge sense of accomplishment, and I did
feel gratified. Every last one of my students, including Pete and Jimmy,
did well enough to pass the class. Pete, in fact, had performed admi-
rably on the multiple-choice aspect of the test, finishing in the top
half of the group. Joe, meanwhile, had earned himself an A- for the
semester.

But the sunny results didn't have me jumping up and down. I was
still on a high from the PowerPoint presentations, which to me delivered the most satisfying moments of the entire semester. Plus I was
preoccupied with my own last-minute assignment.

I needed to hustle over to the library for an end-of-the-year faculty
meeting. Purcell had wanted me to say a few things to all of Mount
Pleasant's teachers, and I had given the opportunity some thought.
But my ideas weren't jelling. I did know that I wasn't inclined to say
much. I believed this show belonged to Mount Pleasant's real teachers, not an interloper like me.

Walking out of room 612 for the last time, I bid farewell to the construction paper shoddily taped to the floor-to-ceiling windows, the big
American flag hanging on the wall, and the speaker box that for six
months had jolted me with a buzzing sound every time class ended.

The library was packed when I arrived. I saw Ellison, Constell,
Nuñez, and many of the other teachers from the social sciences
lounge. There were about a hundred people in the room, some of

whom I'd never met before, or only recognized from passing on the campus or in the parking lot. I managed to push through until I stood next to Wald.

"Where's Delaney?" I whispered.

"Not his scene," Wald whispered back. "He's got his honors students and his classes. I don't think he finds state-of-the-school addresses particularly noteworthy."

Purcell faced his staff, standing in front of a wall with shelves full of reference books. Above him, in big red letters, screamed the word *READ*.

Purcell, as was his custom, did not scream.

"Congratulations on a great year from all of you," he said. "Please give yourselves a round of applause."

Everyone clapped, including Purcell.

Mount Pleasant's principal, dressed in a charcoal blazer and white shirt, seemed energetic. The cusp of summer was a good time to be the school's leader, and Purcell's inextinguishable inner flame was burning bright.

"Our dropout rate held steady, and we had less than two hundred fifty suspensions this year," he said. "That last number is down."

There was modest applause.

"Also, I'll bet that we made strides in school-wide GPA again this year," he added. "Only five years ago, it was less than 2.25. Now we're moving toward 2.8."

I joined in the clapping. I knew how hard-won every gained tenth of a point of GPA could be for teachers and students alike.

"And yet we can do more," Purcell said. "I encourage you all to explore ways to reach your students, to return energized from your summer. We should be on a tireless search to make what we do engaging."

The teachers again applauded. But as staff rallies go, the event was muted. Purcell's encouraging words couldn't overcome his always quiet manner and, more significant, what I sensed as some group-wide frustration. I was in a room full of smart and dedicated professionals. Yet year in and year out, Mount Pleasant's teachers worked with a high volume of students in compromised facilities and under a state-mandated, one-agenda-for-many set of lessons. Purcell himself was hamstrung in his job. He was the captain of a ship, but he didn't hold much sway over the curriculum, or teachers with tenure, or getting a school building's roof patched. The principal tugged at a wheel that wasn't directly connected to a rudder.

I was still wrestling with what I'd say when he asked me to stand before the group.

"For those of you who don't know, Steve Poizner is a successful Silicon Valley entrepreneur and former White House Fellow, and he turned his impressive energies toward one of Mount Pleasant's twelfth-grade American Government classes," said Purcell by way of introduction. "He delivered an inspired spring semester to his students. He brought in guest speakers and writing tutors, and took his kids on field trips and to speak in front of the mayor at City Hall."

Purcell then presented me with a "Rookie Teacher of the Year" certificate. I was honored—and sheepish—about the recognition. I could only imagine what must have been going through some of the teachers' minds: I throw myself at the job, don't I? Where's my recognition?

I kept my speech light. I relived some of my most satisfying moments, and biggest bloopers. I joked about Purcell warning me in the early going that "*They're* hard to handle. *They* can be rude and inconsiderate."

"I thought he was referring to the students," I said during the speech. "But a few weeks later I realized that he was talking to me about some of you teachers."

The laughter that followed my joke was genuine. For once, the comedy muse was with me.

I thanked Wald, Ellison, Constell, Nuñez, and the other social sciences staffers for taking me under their collective wing. They always had answers to my many questions, and often made me feel welcome and supported.

I thanked Purcell profusely. Unlike every other high school principal in the district, he'd given me a chance. He'd recognized that whatever I lacked in experience, I was more than willing to make up for in effort. Purcell had permitted me to walk into a world that I otherwise might never have known. His long career in education had been filled with attempts to improve and even reinvent the learning process, and Project Poizner was right in line with such practices. Take thirty-two American Government seniors and a confirmed risk taker, and what do you get?

"I'm not sure what you all got out of the deal in me coming here," I said to the crowd with a smile. "I know Mount Pleasant gave me a tremendously successful lesson in education."

However, there was one important line that I failed to deliver to that audience. Teaching public school, I'd discovered during my year at Mount Pleasant, was as challenging as any job I'd ever had. In my estimation, teachers are the most underappreciated of all professionals. They work tremendously hard, at jobs that are often thankless. Those words sound clichéd—until you experience the profession firsthand. All I can say is that I wish I'd praised everyone in the library, and asked all the teachers to take a bow.

Part of me was disappointed by Simon Delaney's absence from the faculty gathering. I had thought that maybe as a result of divine intervention or some odd alignment of the planets he would attend the meeting and offer me a hand to shake. I thought this might have been the time and place to see something more positive in the guy.

But such notions were probably fantasy. I think that the whole meeting, and the brave faces put on by Purcell and the rest of the faculty, would have only further soured Delaney. It was probably best that he stayed away.

I couldn't see them clearly. The Mount Pleasant seniors, all dressed in black gowns and mortarboards, were down on the auditorium floor. Meanwhile, I was with many of the teachers, relegated to the balcony of San Jose State University's Event Center. We had bleacher-quality views.

From our vantage point, the kids all looked like dolls, floating as they proceeded in a line toward the stage. Why shouldn't they be walking on air? This was graduation day for the approximately five-hundred-strong Mount Pleasant High School senior class of 2003. Each student glided onto the stage, where Purcell passed out diplomas and shook hands. I knew—I should say I hoped—that all of my students were part of the euphoric group.

Over the noise of cheering parents, family, and friends, I strained to hear the event's master of ceremonies announce the names of my kids over the auditorium's booming sound system.

"Paul Callaway . . . Carol Caneda . . . Tracy Cardenas . . ."

Hooray for Tracy!

"Carlos Formosa . . . Alejandro Francisco . . . Pete Franco . . ."

Pete's dad must be so happy!

"Sue Mah . . . Joel Maloney . . . Donny Mates . . ."

Go Donny!

I was thrilled by what my kids had accomplished, overcoming the challenges that I knew of and those that I likely didn't know about, too. They'd completed a four-year journey, an education odyssey that I was sure some of their parents hadn't completed. Such kids were pioneers in their homes, success stories to be celebrated, cheered, and looked to for a better future.

But, hearing the names called one by one, I wasn't only excited for the kids. I felt chills. I had contributed—at least in a small way—to each of their lives. I'd pushed them to learn more about the country that perhaps their parents weren't yet comfortable calling home. I'd succeeded in helping them get their high school diplomas. And maybe, just maybe, I'd inspired them enough to change their life trajectories, even slightly. Perhaps I gave one kid an ounce more confidence, or another student a widened view of the world. I can certainly hope that I had such an effect, anyway. In education, I do believe that there are individual teachers who dramatically influence their students' lives.

So what would become of Tracy, Pete, Moe, and the rest? Maybe Tracy would become an attorney, and Moe a speechwriter.

Or maybe my students would someday find themselves becoming airplane mechanics, ambulance drivers, ER nurses, and tax processors. Those jobs are as important to California—to any community—as any other jobs. In fact, California's leaders would do well to recognize that schools like Mount Pleasant might flourish by offering other types of education options, too—auto servicing and computer repair, plumbing and woodwork. Vocational ("career") training might keep a heck of a lot more students interested in school. Education providers ought to admit that ever removing vocational training was a mistake.

Watching the kids shake Purcell's hand, I thought about how failing to give them a solid education is to fail ourselves, and our future. The students in my class didn't just belong to their parents. They were children to all of us—society's children, really, meaning we can ill afford to sell even one kid short. What happens if we take twelve years to improve our public schools? We'll lose an entire generation in the process.

I listened again to the names of the graduating students.

"Jorge Rosales . . . Louis Sabedra . . . Jessica Seichu . . ."

Wait a minute, I thought. Where was Komal Saldanha? What had gone wrong? Had she failed another class at Mount Pleasant? Did her dad pull up the stakes and take her east just before graduation? Couldn't he allow his daughter this one moment of glory? Was he thinking about one life, or two?

"Excuse me," said the MC over the loudspeaker. "I missed one.

"Komal Saldanha," he added, and I craned my neck to see a robed figure with a ponytail bouncing in tow.

After the graduation ceremonies ended, I walked onto the auditorium floor. Mortarboards were flying. Music was blaring.

I saw Joe Reardon with his mom and dad. His mother thanked me for my efforts.

I saw Enrique Franco with his arm around Pete, the two of them in the middle of a conversation, laughing.

I spotted Moe Yuen, alone, and wondered if an adult had come to see him receive a diploma.

Finally, I came upon Mrs. Vega and Jimmy.

"Congratulations, Jimmy," I said, shaking his hand. "You've really accomplished something great."

Jimmy's mortarboard was tilted forward on his head, just the way a tough guy would wear it. But nobody can look too macho in a mortarboard, and I don't think he was trying. Jimmy's smile was genuine, like the smile he'd had when we rode next to each other in the bus on our class's first field trip.

"Hey, Mr. Poizner," he said. "You know, you helped me. I noticed."

"Glad we got you through, Jimmy," I said, and nodded and grinned. And then I remembered something.

"Here," I said, and fished a small lapel pin out of my pants pocket. I'd bought it weeks earlier in a surplus store, when I'd been out and about with Carol and Rebecca. The pin was red and blue and said "United States Marine Corps."

I put the pin, still in its packaging, in his right hand.

"Cool," he said, and looked at the pin with genuine appreciation. I waited a few seconds to hear "Thanks," too. But then I reminded myself that Jimmy Vega was a man of few words.

"I wish you a lot of luck, whether you become a marine or try something different," I said. "Whatever you decide, I hope you have a passion for what you do."

Jimmy took one more look at the pin, and then gingerly closed his fingers around it. He wasn't clenching his fist. He wanted to protect something worth saving.

Just Getting Started

Five months after attending Mount Pleasant's graduation, I stood on the steps of another Bay Area school. And on the precipice of another huge challenge.

On a sunny day in November 2003, I launched my political career. Standing in front of Aspire Public Schools' East Palo Alto Charter School, and alongside Doug Purcell, Robert Wald, Reed Hastings, and Don Shalvey, I announced my candidacy for the Republican nomination for the 2004 Twenty-first Assembly District race. I had hoped to win a spot in the state legislature. One big reason for running? Fresh off my experiences at Mount Pleasant, I wanted to start exploring ways to address the education-related agenda that was hot on my mind. After spending much of the year teaching, I'd compiled a healthy list of recommendations for reforming education:

1. **Teachers and principals must have more control of their schools.**

    Unfortunately for California, educators can't make critical decisions about what happens in their classrooms. Teachers' hands are tied behind their backs by the thousands of pages (over one hundred thousand sections) of the state education code. These laws dictate what teachers and principals must do in their schools, as well as when and how they proceed. Moreover, California's system of school financing is unique in that the state government—rather than local authorities—exercises substantial control of the system through which public schools are funded. These practices must change. Decisions concerning money and instruction must be made at local levels. Right now, there is a direct correlation between Sacramento's increased control over California's public schools and the dramatic decline in the state's ability to educate its kids.

2. **The charter school movement should push to expand, in the name of increasing the number of good charter schools *and* positively influencing traditional public schools.**

Charter schools are uniquely positioned to improve the state's public schools. Because they aren't restricted by the dictates of the state education code, charter schools have the freedom and flexibility to innovate in ways that traditional public schools cannot. Therefore charter schools can be highly responsive to their students' needs and in terms of academic performance have already achieved significant results. (Studies have shown that charter schools can dramatically help close the education gap between urban poor and affluent suburban students.) Plus, because they are also publicly funded, charter schools compete directly with traditional public schools for education dollars. The more students a school has, the more money it receives from the state. This competition pushes traditional public schools to vie for students in a constructive way: by improving student outcomes and promoting high-quality teaching.

3. **Pare down public-education bureaucracy in the name of funneling more resources into classrooms.**

   California's public education bureaucracy is glaringly top-heavy. The education system consists of many layers, from the state level to county offices to school districts and finally to individual schools and classrooms. With each level taking a slice of the funding pie, it's easy to see how only a fraction of the tens of billions of dollars originally allocated for "education" actually make their way into the classroom. California's education-funding system should be overhauled so that the money for our public schools does not have to travel such a winding route before it reaches teachers and students. Make *everyone* in education accountable for student performance. Then funding for the programs that successfully improve student outcomes will become a very high priority.

4. **Treat teachers like professionals. Give great teachers great pay and hold all teachers accountable for their work.**

   California's current system of teacher hiring, compensation, and retention fails in two major ways: It doesn't reward the best teachers, and it doesn't discipline the worst teachers. Thus the state's entire teaching profession suffers. In part, this conundrum exists because California's teachers—unlike many other professionals—enjoy enormous amounts of professional protection. And rules reached by collective bargaining agreements create a maze of process and bureaucracy that many school administrators are unwilling to brave. The result is that teachers are rarely fired for shortcomings in their ability to *teach*. If California wants to promote the best practices in the teaching profession while ensuring that every teacher is held accountable for student outcomes, the state should reward its good teachers with higher pay. Bad teachers should be dismissed.

5. **Encourage school principals and their faculties to work creatively, think outside the box, and innovate.**

   California's heavy-handed education code leaves little discretion to the state's "front-line" educators. In other words, teachers aren't encouraged to bring new ideas and thinking into the classroom. Why not strip down the education code to its fundamental goals without mandating *how* teachers and principals—those who know what works and what doesn't—achieve those goals?

6. **Approach the creation of curriculum with the notion that every public school student aspires to achieve. Achievement might mean gaining entrance into a four-year college, receiving excellent vocational training, or getting the very most out of a high-school education.**

   California became the "Golden State" because of its ability to attract a broad range of people with a variety of skills. Unfortunately, the California school system hasn't seized upon this diversity. Instead it has embraced a one-education-fits-all philosophy. That's a mistake. Students must be encouraged to achieve their maximum potential in whatever field they naturally excel in. Future construction workers, health technicians, policemen, and firefighters, for example, are as important to California's future as anyone else. California's public schools should do everything possible to inspire achievement at a variety of pursuits.

7. **Create new paths into the profession of teaching for highly motivated individuals who deserve the opportunity to bring their resources and energy into the classroom.**

   It was nearly impossible for someone like me, who had the time, interest, and determination, to actually teach public-school students.

Giving back shouldn't be so challenging. There are likely hundreds—
if not thousands—of incredible professionals across California who
want to share their knowledge in a classroom. But they can't teach
because thay haven't met a particular set of bureaucratic require-
ments. Schools must be given the flexibility to utilize the human
resources that are all around them. For instance, there should be
programs patterned after what was offered to me at Mount Pleasant,
where a school principal let me teach under the strong supervision
of a trusted, veteren teacher. Individual schools should be given the
flexibility to offer classes to their students at nontraditional times—
like on weekends and after the workday—so that working professionals have the opportunity to share their experiences and expertise
with California's public school students.

Of course, my initial stump speech had to address a few topics:
"Without change, our state government will remain politically unresponsive and fiscally irresponsible," I said at the school-hosted press
conference. "Without relief, our economy will stay hobbled by over-
regulation. Without new ideas, our public schools will continue to fail
our students.

"There are solutions," I added. "There are better times ahead."

As I'd done at Mount Pleasant, I was again about to put myself in
the position of wide-eyed newcomer. Again I would learn a lot, and in
my own style I would do everything within my power to succeed at my
new pursuit of politics. When the campaign hosted parties at private
homes, I stayed until I had answered the last question from the last
remaining guest. My knees got so creaky from walking my district—I
personally knocked on ten thousand doors—that I ultimately slipped
my tiring joints into those stretchy, supportive braces that pro basket-
ball players wear. Meanwhile, I endured Carol's endless chuckles, and

her shrugs, too. For once, she asked me, couldn't I just kick back on the couch and relax?

But Carol and I both know: I'm bad at sitting still. I get the shakes when my BlackBerry goes out of range and rent a second hotel room when Carol, Rebecca, and I take trips together. I actually do relax on family vacations—and then work when everyone else goes to bed.

I won that Republican nomination for the state legislature race, and took my opponent, who was an overwhelming favorite in a historically blue district, to the mat. During that yearlong competition, I learned that I love politics and revel in asking the tough questions about education and other important issues. I had found a second career. When I ultimately lost that race by about 1 percent of the vote, I was only energized to try harder, and in 2006 I was elected California's insurance commissioner. Even then, I knew there were bigger challenges to come.